MW00618435

On
Strategy
(Vol. 2)

HBR's 10 Must Reads series is the definitive collection of ideas and best practices for aspiring and experienced leaders alike. These books offer essential reading selected from the pages of *Harvard Business Review* on topics critical to the success of every manager.

Titles include:

On
Strategy
(Vol. 2)

HARVARD BUSINESS REVIEW PRESS
Boston, Massachusetts

Library of Congress Cataloging-in-Publication Data

Title: HBR's 10 must reads. Vol. 2 : on strategy.
Other titles: On strategy. Vol. 2. | HBR's 10 must reads (Series)
Description: Boston, Massachusetts : Harvard Business Review Press, [2020]
    | Series: HBR's 10 must reads | Includes index.
Identifiers: LCCN 2019043387 (print) | LCCN 2019043388 (ebook) | ISBN
    9781633699168 (paperback) | ISBN 9781633699175 (ebook)
Subjects: LCSH: Strategic planning.
Classification: LCC HD30.28 .H3953 2020 (print) | LCC HD30.28 (ebook) |
    DDC 658.4/012—dc23
LC record available at https://lccn.loc.gov/2019043387
LC ebook record available at https://lccn.loc.gov/2019043388

ISBN: 978-1-63369-916-8
eISBN: 978-1-63369-917-5

Contents

Your Strategy Needs a Strategy

by Martin Reeves, Claire Love, and Philipp Tillmanns

THE OIL INDUSTRY HOLDS RELATIVELY few surprises for strategists. Things change, of course, sometimes dramatically, but in relatively predictable ways. Planners know, for instance, that global supply will rise and fall as geopolitical forces play out and new resources are discovered and exploited. They know that demand will rise and fall with incomes, GDPs, weather conditions, and the like. Because these factors are outside companies' and their competitors' control and barriers to entry are so high, no one is really in a position to change the game much. A company carefully marshals its unique capabilities and resources to stake out and defend its competitive position in this fairly stable firmament.

The internet software industry would be a nightmare for an oil industry strategist. Innovations and new companies pop up frequently, seemingly out of nowhere, and the pace at which companies can build—or lose—volume and market share is head-spinning. A major player like Microsoft or Google or Facebook can, without much warning, introduce some new platform or standard that fundamentally alters the basis of competition. In this environment, competitive advantage comes from reading and responding to signals faster than your rivals do, adapting quickly to change, or capitalizing on technological leadership to influence how demand and competition evolve.

When the Cold Winds Blow

THERE ARE CIRCUMSTANCES in which none of our strategic styles will work well: when access to capital or other critical resources is severely restricted, by either a sharp economic downturn or some other cataclysmic event. Such a harsh environment threatens the very viability of a company and demands a fifth strategic style—*survival*.

As its name implies, a survival strategy requires a company to focus defensively—reducing costs, preserving capital, trimming business portfolios. It is a short-term strategy, intended to clear the way for the company to live another day. But it does not lead to any long-term growth strategy. Companies in survival mode should therefore look ahead, readying themselves to assess the conditions of the new environment and to adopt an appropriate growth strategy once the crisis ends.

Clearly, the kinds of strategies that would work in the oil industry have practically no hope of working in the far less predictable and far less settled arena of internet software. And the skill sets that oil and software strategists need are worlds apart as well, because they operate on different time scales, use different tools, and have very different relationships with the people on the front lines who implement their plans. Companies operating in such dissimilar competitive environments should be planning, developing, and deploying their strategies in markedly different ways. But all too often, our research shows, they are not.

That is not for want of trying. Responses from a recent BCG survey of 120 companies around the world in 10 major industry sectors show that executives are well aware of the need to match their strategy-making processes to the specific demands of their competitive environments. Still, the survey found, in practice many rely instead on approaches that are better suited to predictable, stable environments, even when their own environments are known to be highly volatile or mutable.

What's stopping these executives from making strategy in a way that fits their situation? We believe they lack a systematic way to go about it—a strategy for making strategy. Here we present a simple framework that divides strategy planning into four styles according to how predictable your environment is and how much power

Idea in Brief

Companies that correctly match their strategy-making processes to their competitive circumstances perform better than those that don't. But too many use approaches appropriate only to predictable environments—even in highly volatile situations.

What executives in these cases need is a strategy for setting strategy. The authors present a framework for choosing one, which begins with two questions: How unpredictable is your environment? and How much power do you or others have to change that environment?

The answers give rise to four broad strategic styles, each one particularly suited to a distinct environment.

- **A classical strategy** (the one everyone learned in business school) works well for companies operating in predictable and immutable environments.

- **An adaptive strategy** is more flexible and experimental and works far better in immutable environments that are unpredictable.

- **A shaping strategy** is best in unpredictable environments that you have the power to change.

- **A visionary strategy** (the build-it-and-they-will-come approach) is appropriate in predictable environments that you have the power to change.

you have to change it. Using this framework, corporate leaders can match their strategic style to the particular conditions of their industry, business function, or geographic market.

How you set your strategy constrains the kind of strategy you develop. With a clear understanding of the strategic styles available and the conditions under which each is appropriate, more companies can do what we have found that the most successful are already doing—deploying their unique capabilities and resources to better capture the opportunities available to them.

Finding the Right Strategic Style

Strategy usually begins with an assessment of your industry. Your choice of strategic style should begin there as well. Although many industry factors will play into the strategy you actually formulate, you can narrow down your options by considering just two critical factors: *predictability* (How far into the future and how accurately can you confidently forecast demand, corporate performance, competitive dynamics, and market expectations?) and *malleability* (To what extent can you or your competitors influence those factors?).

Put these two variables into a matrix, and four broad strategic styles—which we label *classical, adaptive, shaping,* and *visionary*—emerge. (See the exhibit "The right strategic style for your environment.") Each style is associated with distinct planning practices and is best suited to one environment. Too often strategists conflate predictability and malleability—thinking that any environment that can be shaped is unpredictable—and thus divide the world of strategic possibilities into only two parts (predictable and immutable or unpredictable and mutable), whereas they ought to consider all four. So it did not surprise us to find that companies that match their strategic style to their environment perform significantly better than those that don't. In our analysis, the three-year total shareholder returns of companies in our survey that use the right style were 4% to 8% higher, on average, than the returns of those that do not.

Let's look at each style in turn.

Classical

When you operate in an industry whose environment is predictable but hard for your company to change, a classical strategic style has the best chance of success. This is the style familiar to most managers and business school graduates—five forces, blue ocean, and growth-share matrix analyses are all manifestations of it. A company sets a goal, targeting the most favorable market position it can attain by capitalizing on its particular capabilities and resources, and then tries to build and fortify that position through orderly, successive rounds of planning, using quantitative predictive methods that allow it to project well into the future. Once such plans are set, they tend to stay in place for several years. Classical strategic planning can work well as a stand-alone function because it requires special

The right strategic style for your environment

Our research shows that approaches to strategy formulation fall into four buckets, according to how predictable an industry's environment is and how easily companies can change that environment.

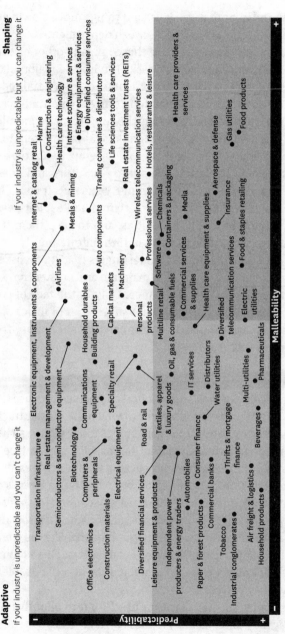

Adaptive
If your industry is unpredictable and you can't change it

Shaping
If your industry is unpredictable but you can change it

Classical
If your industry is predictable but you can't change it

Visionary
If your industry is predictable and you can change it

Predictability

Malleability

Source: **BCG analysis**

analytic and quantitative skills, and things move slowly enough to allow for information to pass between departments.

Oil company strategists, like those in many other mature industries, effectively employ the classical style. At a major oil company such as ExxonMobil or Shell, for instance, highly trained analysts in the corporate strategic-planning office spend their days developing detailed perspectives on the long-term economic factors relating to demand and the technological factors relating to supply. These analyses allow them to devise upstream oil-extraction plans that may stretch 10 years into the future and downstream production-capacity plans up to five years out. It could hardly be otherwise, given the time needed to find and exploit new sources of oil, to build production facilities, and to keep them running at optimum capacity. These plans, in turn, inform multiyear financial forecasts, which determine annual targets that are focused on honing the efficiencies required to maintain and bolster the company's market position and performance. Only in the face of something extraordinary—an extended Gulf war; a series of major oil refinery shutdowns—would plans be seriously revisited more frequently than once a year.

Adaptive

The classical approach works for oil companies because their strategists operate in an environment in which the most attractive positions and the most rewarded capabilities today will, in all likelihood, remain the same tomorrow. But that has never been true for some industries, and, as has been noted before in these pages ("Adaptability: The New Competitive Advantage," by Martin Reeves and Mike Deimler, HBR, July–August 2011), it's becoming less and less true where global competition, technological innovation, social feedback loops, and economic uncertainty combine to make the environment radically and persistently unpredictable. In such an environment, a carefully crafted classical strategy may become obsolete within months or even weeks.

Companies in this situation need a more adaptive approach, whereby they can constantly refine goals and tactics and shift, acquire, or divest resources smoothly and promptly. In such a fast-moving, reactive environment, when predictions are likely to be wrong and long-term plans are essentially useless, the goal cannot be to optimize efficiency; rather, it must be to engineer flexibility. Accordingly, planning cycles may shrink to less than a year or even become continual. Plans take the form not of carefully specified blueprints but of rough hypotheses based on the best available data. In testing them out, strategy must be tightly linked with or embedded in operations, to best capture change signals and minimize information loss and time lags.

Specialty fashion retailing is a good example of this. Tastes change quickly. Brands become hot (or not) overnight. No amount of data or planning will grant fashion executives the luxury of knowing far in advance what to make. So their best bet is to set up their organizations to continually produce, roll out, and test a variety of products as quickly as they can, constantly adapting production in the light of new learning.

The Spanish retailer Zara uses the adaptive approach. Zara does not rely heavily on a formal planning process; rather, its strategic style is baked into its flexible supply chain. It maintains strong ties with its 1,400 external suppliers, which work closely with its designers and marketers. As a result, Zara can design, manufacture, and ship a garment to its stores in as little as two to three weeks, rather than the industry average of four to six months. This allows the company to experiment with a wide variety of looks and make small bets with small batches of potentially popular styles. If they prove a hit, Zara can ramp up production quickly. If they don't, not much is lost in markdowns. (On average, Zara marks down only 15% of its inventory, whereas the figure for competitors can be as high as 50%.) So it need not predict or make bets on which fashions will capture its customers' imaginations and wallets from month to month. Instead it can respond quickly to information from its retail stores, constantly experiment with various offerings, and smoothly adjust to events as they play out.

Zara's strategic style requires relationships among its planners, designers, manufacturers, and distributors that are entirely different from what a company like ExxonMobil needs. Nevertheless, Exxon's strategists and Zara's designers have one critical thing in common: They take their competitive environment as a given and aim to carve out the best place they can within it.

Shaping

Some environments, as internet software vendors well know, can't be taken as given. For instance, in new or young high-growth industries where barriers to entry are low, innovation rates are high, demand is very hard to predict, and the relative positions of competitors are in flux, a company can often radically shift the course of industry development through some innovative move. A mature industry that's similarly fragmented and not dominated by a few powerful incumbents, or is stagnant and ripe for disruption, is also likely to be similarly malleable.

In such an environment, a company employing a classical or even an adaptive strategy to find the best possible market position runs the risk of selling itself short, being overrun by events, and missing opportunities to control its own fate. It would do better to employ a strategy in which the goal is to shape the unpredictable environment to its own advantage before someone else does—so that it benefits no matter how things play out.

Like an adaptive strategy, a shaping strategy embraces short or continual planning cycles. Flexibility is paramount, little reliance is placed on elaborate prediction mechanisms, and the strategy is most commonly implemented as a portfolio of experiments. But unlike adapters, shapers focus beyond the boundaries of their own company, often by rallying a formidable ecosystem of customers, suppliers, and/or complementors to their cause by defining attractive new markets, standards, technology platforms, and business practices. They propagate these through marketing, lobbying, and savvy partnerships. In the early stages of the digital revolution, internet software companies frequently used shaping strategies to create new communities, standards, and platforms that became the foundations for new markets and businesses.

That's essentially how Facebook overtook the incumbent MySpace in just a few years. One of Facebook's savviest strategic moves was to open its social-networking platform to outside developers in 2007, thus attracting all manner of applications to its site. Facebook couldn't hope to predict how big or successful any one of them would become. But it didn't need to. By 2008 it had attracted 33,000 applications; by 2010 that number had risen to more than 550,000. So as the industry developed and more than two-thirds of the successful social-networking apps turned out to be games, it was not surprising that the most popular ones—created by Zynga, Playdom, and Playfish—were operating from, and enriching, Facebook's site. What's more, even if the social-networking landscape shifts dramatically as time goes on, chances are the most popular applications will still be on Facebook. That's because by creating a flexible and popular platform, the company actively shaped the business environment to its own advantage rather than merely staking out a position in an existing market or reacting to changes, however quickly, after they'd occurred.

Visionary

Sometimes, not only does a company have the power to shape the future, but it's possible to know that future and to predict the path to realizing it. Those times call for bold strategies—the kind entrepreneurs use to create entirely new markets (as Edison did for electricity and Martine Rothblatt did for XM satellite radio), or corporate leaders use to revitalize a company with a wholly new vision—as Ratan Tata is trying to do with the ultra-affordable Nano automobile. These are the big bets, the build-it-and-they-will-come strategies.

Like a shaping strategist, the visionary considers the environment not as a given but as something that can be molded to advantage. Even so, the visionary style has more in common with a classical than with an adaptive approach. Because the goal is clear, strategists can take deliberate steps to reach it without having to keep many options open. It's more important for them to take the time and care they need to marshal resources, plan thoroughly, and implement correctly so that the vision doesn't fall victim to poor execution. Visionary strategists must have the courage to stay the course and the will to commit the necessary resources.

Back in 1994, for example, it became clear to UPS that the rise of internet commerce was going to be a bonanza for delivery companies, because the one thing online retailers would always need was a way to get their offerings out of cyberspace and onto their customers' doorsteps. This future may have been just as clear to the much younger and smaller FedEx, but UPS had the means—and the will—to make the necessary investments. That year it set up a cross-functional committee drawn from IT, sales, marketing, and finance to map out its path to becoming what the company later called "the enablers of global e-commerce." The committee identified the ambitious initiatives that UPS would need to realize this vision, which involved investing some $1 billion a year to integrate its core package-tracking operations with those of web providers and make acquisitions to expand its global delivery capacity. By 2000 UPS's multibillion-dollar bet had paid off: The company had snapped up a whopping 60% of the e-commerce delivery market.

Avoiding the Traps

In our survey, fully three out of four executives understood that they needed to employ different strategic styles in different circumstances. Yet judging by the practices they actually adopted, we estimate that the same percentage were using only the two strategic styles—classic and visionary—suited to predictable environments (see the exhibit "Which strategic style is used the most?"). That means only one in four was prepared in practice to adapt to unforeseeable events or to seize an opportunity to shape an industry to his or her company's advantage. Given our analysis of how unpredictable their business environments actually are, this number is far too low. Understanding how different the various approaches are and in which environment each best applies can go a long way toward correcting mismatches between strategic style and business environment. But as strategists think through the implications of the framework, they need to avoid three traps we have frequently observed.

Misplaced confidence
You can't choose the right strategic style unless you accurately judge how predictable and malleable your environment is. But when we

Which strategic style is used the most?

Our survey found that companies were most often using the two styles best suited to predictable environments—classical and visionary—even when their environments were clearly unpredictable.

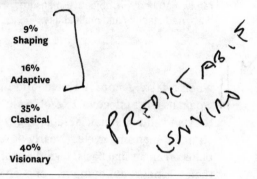

9%
Shaping

16%
Adaptive

35%
Classical

40%
Visionary

compared executives' perceptions with objective measures of their actual environments, we saw a strong tendency to overestimate both factors. Nearly half the executives believed they could control uncertainty in the business environment through their own actions. More than 80% said that achieving goals depended on their own actions more than on things they could not control.

Unexamined habits

Many executives recognized the importance of building the adaptive capabilities required to address unpredictable environments, but fewer than one in five felt sufficiently competent in them. In part that's because many executives learned only the classical style, through experience or at business school. Accordingly, we weren't surprised to find that nearly 80% said that in practice they begin their strategic planning by articulating a goal and then analyzing how best to get there. What's more, some 70% said that in practice they value accuracy over speed of decisions, even when they are well aware that their environment is fast-moving and unpredictable. As a result, a lot of time is being wasted making untenable predictions

Are You Clinging to the Wrong Strategy Style?

A CLEAR ESTIMATION of your industry's predictability and malleability is key to picking the right strategy style. But our survey of more than 120 companies in 10 industries showed that companies don't do this well: Their estimates rarely matched our objective measures. They consistently *overestimated* both predictability and malleability.

when a faster, more iterative, and more experimental approach would be more effective. Executives are also closely attuned to quarterly and annual financial reporting, which heavily influences their strategic-planning cycles. Nearly 90% said they develop strategic plans on an annual basis, regardless of the actual pace of change in their business environments—or even what they perceive it to be.

Culture mismatches

Although many executives recognize the importance of adaptive capabilities, it can be highly countercultural to implement them. Classical strategies aimed at achieving economies of scale and scope often create company cultures that prize efficiency and the elimination of variation. These can of course undermine the opportunity to experiment and learn, which is essential for an adaptive strategy. And failure is a natural outcome of experimentation, so adaptive and shaping strategies fare poorly in cultures that punish it.

Avoiding some of these traps can be straightforward once the differing requirements of the four strategic styles are understood. Simply being aware that adaptive planning horizons don't necessarily correlate well with the rhythms of financial markets, for instance, might go a long way toward eliminating ingrained planning habits. Similarly, understanding that the point of shaping and visionary strategies is to change the game rather than to optimize your position in the market may be all that's needed to avoid starting with the wrong approach.

Being more thoughtful about metrics is also helpful. Although companies put a great deal of energy into making predictions year after year, it's surprising how rarely they check to see if the predictions they made in the prior year actually panned out. We suggest regularly reviewing the accuracy of your forecasts and also objectively gauging predictability by tracking how often and to what extent companies in your industry change relative position in terms of revenue, profitability, and other performance measures. To get a better sense of the extent to which industry players can change their environment, we recommend measuring industry youthfulness, concentration, growth rate, innovation rate, and rate of technology change—all of which increase malleability.

Operating in Many Modes

Matching your company's strategic style to the predictability and malleability of your industry will align overall strategy with the broad economic conditions in which the company operates. But various company units may well operate in differing subsidiary or geographic markets that are more or less predictable and malleable than the industry at large. Strategists in these units and markets can use the same process to select the most effective style for their particular circumstances, asking themselves the same initial questions: How predictable is the environment in which our unit operates? How much power do we have to change that environment? The answers may vary widely. We estimate, for example, that the Chinese business environment overall has been almost twice as malleable and unpredictable as that in the United States, making shaping strategies often more appropriate in China.

Similarly, the functions within your company are likely to operate in environments that call for differing approaches to departmental planning. It's easy to imagine, for instance, that within the auto industry a classical style would work well for optimizing production but would be inappropriate for the digital marketing department, which probably has a far greater power to shape its environment (after all, that's what advertising aims to do) and would hardly benefit from mapping out its campaigns years in advance.

The Ultimate in Strategic Flexibility

HAIER, A CHINESE HOME-APPLIANCE MANUFACTURER, may have taken strategic flexibility just about as far as it can go. The company has devised a system in which units as small as an individual can effectively use differing styles.

How does it manage this? Haier's organization comprises thousands of minicompanies, each accountable for its own P&L. Any employee can start one of them. But there are no cost centers in the company—only profit centers. Each minicompany bears the fully loaded costs of its operations, and each party negotiates with the others for services; even the finance department sells its services to the others. Every employee is held accountable for achieving profits. An employee's salary is based on a simple formula: base salary × % of monthly target achieved + bonus (or deduction) based on individual P&L. In other words, if a minicompany achieves none of its monthly target (0%), the employees in it receive no salary that month.

Operating at this level of flexibility can be as rewarding as it is daunting. Near bankruptcy in 1985, Haier has since become the world's largest home-appliance company—ahead of LG, Samsung, GE, and Whirlpool.

If units or functions within your company would benefit from operating in a strategic style other than the one best suited to your industry as a whole, it follows that you will very likely need to manage more than one strategic style at a time. Executives in our survey are well aware of this: In fact, fully 90% aspired to improve their ability to manage multiple styles simultaneously. The simplest but also the least flexible way to do this is to structure and run functions, regions, or business units that require differing strategic styles separately. Allowing teams within units to select their own styles gives you more flexibility in diverse or fast-changing environments but is generally more challenging to realize. (For an example of a company that has found a systematic way to do it, see the sidebar "The Ultimate in Strategic Flexibility.")

Finally, a company moving into a different stage of its life cycle may well require a shift in strategic style. Environments for start-ups tend to be malleable, calling for visionary or shaping strategies. In a company's growth and maturity phases, when the environment is less malleable, adaptive or classical styles are often best. For companies in a declining phase, the environment becomes more malleable again, generating opportunities for disruption and rejuvenation through either a shaping or a visionary strategy.

Once you have correctly analyzed your environment, not only for the business as a whole but for each of your functions, divisions, and geographic markets, and you have identified which strategic styles should be used, corrected for your own biases, and taken steps to prime your company's culture so that the appropriate styles can successfully be applied, you will need to monitor your environment and be prepared to adjust as conditions change over time. Clearly that's no easy task. But we believe that companies that continually match their strategic styles to their situation will enjoy a tremendous advantage over those that don't.

Originally published in September 2012. Reprint R1209E

Transient Advantage

by Rita Gunther McGrath

STRATEGY IS STUCK. For too long the business world has been obsessed with the notion of building a sustainable competitive advantage. That idea is at the core of most strategy textbooks; it forms the basis of Warren Buffett's investment strategy; it's central to the success of companies on the "most admired" lists. I'm not arguing that it's a bad idea—obviously, it's marvelous to compete in a way that others can't imitate. And even today there are companies that create a strong position and defend it for extended periods of time—firms such as GE, IKEA, Unilever, Tsingtao Brewery, and Swiss Re. But it's now rare for a company to maintain a truly lasting advantage. Competitors and customers have become too unpredictable, and industries too amorphous. The forces at work here are familiar: the digital revolution, a "flat" world, fewer barriers to entry, globalization.

Strategy *is* still useful in turbulent industries like consumer electronics, fast-moving consumer goods, television, publishing, photography, and . . . well, you get the idea. Leaders in these businesses can compete effectively—but not by sticking to the same old playbook. In a world where a competitive advantage often evaporates in less than a year, companies can't afford to spend months at a time crafting a single long-term strategy. To stay ahead, they need to constantly start new strategic initiatives, building and exploiting many *transient competitive advantages* at once. Though individually temporary, these advantages, as a portfolio, can keep companies in the lead over the long run. Firms that have figured this out—such as

Milliken & Company, a U.S.-based textiles and chemicals company; Cognizant, a global IT services company; and Brambles, a logistics company based in Australia—have abandoned the assumption that stability in business is the norm. They don't even think it should be a goal. Instead, they work to spark continuous change, avoiding dangerous rigidity. They view strategy differently—as more fluid, more customer-centric, less industry-bound. And the ways they formulate it—the lens they use to define the competitive playing field, their methods for evaluating new business opportunities, their approach to innovation—are different as well.

I'm hardly the first person to write about how fast-moving competition changes strategy; indeed, I'm building on the work of Ian MacMillan (a longtime coauthor), Kathleen Eisenhardt, Yves Doz, George Stalk, Mikko Kosonen, Richard D'Aveni, Paul Nunes, and others. However, the thinking in this area—and the reality on the ground—has reached an inflection point. The field of strategy needs to acknowledge what a multitude of practitioners already know: Sustainable competitive advantage is now the exception, not the rule. Transient advantage is the new normal.

The Anatomy of a Transient Advantage

Any competitive advantage—whether it lasts two seasons or two decades—goes through the same life cycle. (See "The wave of transient advantage.") But when advantages are fleeting, firms must rotate through the cycle much more quickly and more often, so they need a deeper understanding of the early and late stages than they would if they were able to maintain one strong position for many years.

A competitive advantage begins with a *launch* process, in which the organization identifies an opportunity and mobilizes resources to capitalize on it. In this phase a company needs people who are capable of filling in blank sheets of paper with ideas, who are comfortable with experimentation and iteration, and who probably get bored with the kind of structure required to manage a large, complex organization.

Idea in Brief

The dominant idea in the field of strategy—that success consists of establishing a unique competitive position, sustained for long periods of time—is no longer relevant for most businesses. They need to embrace the notion of transient advantage instead, learning to launch new strategic initiatives again and again, and creating a portfolio of advantages that can be built quickly and abandoned just as rapidly. Success will require a new set of operational capabilities.

In the next phase, *ramp up,* the business idea is brought to scale. This period calls for people who can assemble the right resources at the right time with the right quality and deliver on the promise of the idea.

Then, if a firm is fortunate, it begins a period of *exploitation,* in which it captures profits and share, and forces competitors to react. At this point a company needs people who are good at M&A, analytical decision making, and efficiency. Traditional established companies have plenty of talent with this skill set.

Often, the very success of the initiative spawns competition, weakening the advantage. So the firm has to *reconfigure* what it's doing to keep the advantage fresh. For reconfigurations, a firm needs people who aren't afraid to radically rethink business models or resources.

In some cases the advantage is completely eroded, compelling the company to begin a *disengagement* process in which resources are extracted and reallocated to the next-generation advantage. To manage this process, you need people who can be candid and tough-minded and can make emotionally difficult decisions.

For sensible reasons, companies with any degree of maturity tend to be oriented toward the exploitation phase of the life cycle. But as I've suggested, they need different skills, metrics, and people to manage the tasks inherent in each stage of an advantage's development. And if they're creating a pipeline of competitive advantages, the challenge is even more complex, because they'll need to orchestrate many activities that are inconsistent with one another.

Milliken & Company is a fascinating example of an organization that managed to overcome the competitive forces that annihilated its industry (albeit over a longer time period than some companies

The wave of transient advantage

Companies in high-velocity industries must learn to cycle rapidly through the stages of competitive advantage. They also need the capacity to develop and manage a pipeline of initiatives, since many will be short-lived.

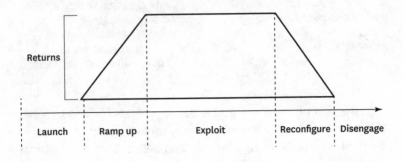

today will be granted). By 1991 virtually all of Milliken's traditional competitors had vanished, victims of a surge in global competition that moved the entire business of textile manufacturing to Asia. In Milliken, one sees very clearly the pattern of entering new, more promising arenas while disengaging from older, exhausted ones. Ultimately, the company exited most of its textile lines, but it did not do so suddenly. It gradually shut down American plants, starting in the 1980s and continuing through 2009. (Every effort was made, as best I can tell, to reallocate workers who might have suffered as a result.) At the same time the company was investing in international expansion, new technologies, and new markets, including forays into new arenas to which its capabilities provided access. As a result, a company that had been largely focused on textiles and chemicals through the 1960s, and advanced materials and flameproof products through the 1990s, had become a leader in specialty materials and high-IP specialty chemicals by the 2000s.

Facing the Brutal Truth

In a world that values exploitation, people on the front lines are rarely rewarded for telling powerful senior executives that a competitive advantage is fading away. Better to shore up an existing advantage for as long as possible, until the pain becomes so obvious that there is no choice. That's what happened at IBM, Sony, Nokia, Kodak, and a host of other firms that got themselves into terrible trouble, despite ample early warnings from those working with customers.

To compete in a transient-advantage economy, you must be willing to honestly assess whether current advantages are at risk. Ask yourself which of these statements is true of your company:

- I don't buy my own company's products or services.

- We're investing at the same or higher levels and not getting better margins or growth in return.

- Customers are finding cheaper or simpler solutions to be "good enough."

- Competition is emerging from places we didn't expect.

- Customers are no longer excited about what we have to offer.

- We're not considered a top place to work by the people we'd like to hire.

- Some of our very best people are leaving.

- Our stock is perpetually undervalued.

If you nodded in agreement with four or more of these, that's a clear warning that you may be facing imminent erosion.

But it isn't enough to recognize a problem. You also have to abandon many of the traditional notions about competitive strategy that will exacerbate the challenge of strategy reinvention.

Seven Dangerous Misconceptions

Most executives working in a high-velocity setting know perfectly well that they need to change their mode of operation. Often, though, deeply embedded assumptions can lead companies into traps. Here are the ones I see most often.

The first-mover trap

This is the belief that being first to market and owning assets create a sustainable position. In some businesses—like aircraft engines or mining—that's still true. But in most industries a first-mover advantage doesn't last.

The superiority trap

Almost any early-stage technology, process, or product won't be as effective as something that's been honed and polished for years. Because of that disparity, many companies don't see the need to invest in improving their established offerings—until the upstart innovations mature, by which time it's often too late for the incumbents.

The quality trap

Many businesses in exploit mode stick with a level of quality higher than customers are prepared to pay for. When a cheaper, simpler offer is good enough, customers will abandon the incumbent.

The hostage-resources trap

In most companies, executives running big, profitable businesses get to call the shots. These people have no incentive to shift resources to new ventures. I remember holding a Nokia product that was remarkably similar to today's iPad—in about 2004. It hooked up to the internet, accessed web pages, and even had a rudimentary app constellation. Why did Nokia never capitalize on this ground-breaking innovation? Because the company's emphasis was on mass-market phones, and resource allocation decisions were made accordingly.

The white-space trap

When I ask executives about the biggest barriers to innovation, I often hear, "Well, these things fall between the cracks of our organizational structure." When opportunities don't fit their structure, firms often simply forgo them instead of making the effort to reorganize. For instance, a product manufacturer might pass up potentially profitable moves into services because they require coordination of activities along a customer's experience, rather than by product line.

The empire-building trap

In a lot of companies, the more assets and employees you manage, the better. This system promotes hoarding, bureaucracy building, and fierce defense of the status quo; it inhibits experimentation, iterative learning, and risk taking. And it causes employees who like to do new things to leave.

The sporadic-innovation trap

Many companies do not have a system for creating a pipeline of new advantages. As a result, innovation is an on-again, off-again process that is driven by individuals, making it extraordinarily vulnerable to swings in the business cycle.

The assessment "Is Your Company Prepared for the Transient-Advantage Economy?" at the end of this chapter will give you a sense of whether your organization is vulnerable to these traps.

Strategy for Transient Advantage: The New Playbook

Companies that want to create a portfolio of transient advantages need to make eight major shifts in the way that they operate.

1. Think about arenas, not industries

One of the more cherished ideas in traditional management is that by looking at data about other firms like yours, you can uncover the right strategy for your organization. Indeed, one of the most influential strategy frameworks, Michael Porter's five forces model, assumes that you are mainly comparing your company to others in a similar industry. In today's environment, where industry lines are quickly blurring, this can blindside you.

I've seen untraditional competitors take companies by surprise over and over again. In the 1980s, for instance, no money-center bank even saw the threat posed by Merrill Lynch's new cash-management accounts, because they weren't offered by any bank.

Millions in deposits flew out the door before the banks realized what was going on. But in recent years, the phenomenon has become more common. Google's moves into phone operating systems and online video have created consternation in traditional phone businesses; retailers like Walmart have begun edging into health care; and the entire activity of making payments is being disrupted by players from a variety of industries, including mobile phone operators, internet credit providers, and swipe-card makers.

Today strategy involves orchestrating competitive moves in what I call "arenas." An arena is a combination of a customer segment, an offer, and a place in which that offer is delivered. It isn't that industries aren't relevant anymore; it's just that industry-level analysis doesn't give you the full picture. Indeed, the very notion of a transient competitive advantage is less about making more money than your industry peers, as conventional definitions would have it, and more about responding to customers' "jobs to be done" (as Tony Ulwick would call it) in a given space.

2. Set broad themes, and then let people experiment

The shift to a focus on arenas means that you can't analyze your way to an advantage with armies of junior staffers or consultants anymore. Today's gifted strategists examine the data, certainly, but they also use advanced pattern recognition, direct observation, and the interpretation of weak signals in the environment to set broad themes. Within those themes, they free people to try different approaches and business models. Cognizant, for instance, clearly spells out the competitive terrain it would like to claim but permits people on the ground considerable latitude within that framework. "The Future of Work" is Cognizant's umbrella term for a host of services intended to help clients rethink their business models, reinvent their workforces, and rewire their operations—all with the firm's assistance, of course.

3. Adopt metrics that support entrepreneurial growth

When advantages come and go, conventional metrics can effectively kill off innovations by imposing decision rules that make no sense. The net present value rule, for instance, assumes that you will complete every project you start, that advantages will last for quite a while, and that there will even be a "terminal value" left once they are gone. It leads companies to underinvest in new opportunities.

Instead, firms can use the logic of "real options" to evaluate new moves. A real option is a small investment that conveys the right, but not the obligation, to make a more significant commitment in the future. It allows the organization to learn through trial and error. Consider the way Intuit has made experimentation a core strategic process, amplifying by orders of magnitude its ability to venture into new spaces and try new things. As Kaaren Hanson, the company's vice president of design innovation, said at a recent conference at Columbia Business School, the important thing is to "fall in love with the problem you are trying to solve" rather than with the solution, and to be comfortable with iteration as you work toward the answer.

4. Focus on experiences and solutions to problems

As barriers to entry tumble, product features can be copied in an instant. Even service offerings in many industries have become commoditized. Once a company has demonstrated that demand for something exists, competitors quickly move in. What customers crave—and few companies provide—are well-designed experiences and complete solutions to their problems. Unfortunately, many companies are so internally focused that they're oblivious to the customer's experience. You call up your friendly local cable company or telephone provider and get connected to a robot. The robot wants to know your customer number, which you dutifully provide. Eventually, the robot decides that your particular problem is too difficult and hands you over to a live person. What's the first thing the person wants to know? Yup, your customer number. It's symptomatic of the disjointed and fragmented way most complex organizations handle customers.

Companies skilled at exploiting transient advantage put themselves in their customers' place and consider the outcome customers are trying to achieve. Australia's Brambles has done a really great job of this even though it is in a seemingly dull industry (managing the logistics of pallets and other containers). The company realized that one of grocers' biggest costs was the labor required to shelve goods delivered to their stores. Brambles designed a solution: plastic bins that can be filled by growers right in the fields and lifted directly from pallets and placed on shelves, from which customers can help themselves. It has cut labor costs significantly. Better yet, fruits and vegetables arrive at the point of purchase in better shape because they aren't manhandled repeatedly as they go from field to box to truck to warehouse to storage room to shelf. Although seemingly low-tech, this initiative and others like it have generated substantial profits and steady growth for the company—not to mention customers' appreciation.

5. Build strong relationships and networks

One of the few barriers to entry that remain powerful in a transient-advantage context has to do with people and their personal networks. Indeed, evidence suggests that the most successful and sought-after employees are those with the most robust networks. Realizing that strong relationships with customers are a profound source of advantage, many companies have begun to invest in communities and networks as a way of deepening ties with customers. Intuit, for example, has created a space on its website where customers can interact, solve one another's problems, and share ideas. The company goes so far as to recognize exemplary problem solvers with special titles and short profiles of them on the site. Amazon and TripAdvisor both make contributions from their communities a core part of the value they offer customers. And of course, social networks have the power to enhance or destroy a firm's credibility in nanoseconds as customers enjoy an unprecedented ability to connect with one another.

Firms that are skilled at managing networks are also notable for the way they preserve important relationships. Infosys, for instance, is choosy about which customers it will serve, but it maintains a 97% customer retention rate. Sagentia, a technical consultancy in the UK, is extremely conscientious about making sure that people who are let go remain on good terms with the firm and land well in new positions. Even at a large industrial company like GE, the senior leaders spend inordinate amounts of time building and preserving relationships with other firms.

6. Avoid brutal restructuring; learn healthy disengagement

In researching firms that effectively navigate the transient-advantage economy, I was struck by how seldom they engaged in restructuring, downsizing, or mass firings. Instead, many of them seemed to continually adjust and readjust their resources. At Infosys, I was told, people don't really believe in "chopping things off." Rather, when an initiative is wound down, they say it "finds its way to insignificance."

Sometimes, of course, downsizing or sudden shifts can't be avoided. The challenge then is disengaging from a business in the least destructive, most beneficial way. Netflix's efforts to get out of the DVD-shipping business and into streaming movies, which its management passionately believes represents the future, offer an interesting lesson in the wrong way to do this. In 2011 the company's management made two decisions that infuriated customers. It imposed a massive price increase across the board, and it split the DVD and streaming businesses into two separate organizations, which forced customers to duplicate their efforts to find and purchase movies. Let's assume that Netflix's leaders are right that eventually the DVD part of the business will shrivel up. How might the firm have exited more gracefully?

Preparing customers to transition away from old advantages is a lot like getting them to adopt a new product, but in reverse. Not all customers will be prepared to move at the same rate. There is a sequence to which customers you should transition first, second, and so on.

If, rather than raising prices for everybody, Netflix had selectively offered price discounts to those who would drop the DVD service, it would have moved that segment over to the new model. Then it could have gone to the "light user" DVD consumers and suggested that instead of getting a new DVD anytime they wanted it, they would get one once a month, say, for the same price. If they wanted the instant service, their prices would go up. That would shift another group to lower DVD usage. Then when those segments started to realize that all-streaming wasn't so bad, Netflix could have instituted the big price increase for the mainstream buyer. The point is that in trying to force many customers to move faster than they were prepared to, the company enraged them.

7. Get systematic about early-stage innovation

If advantages eventually disappear, it only makes sense to have a process for filling your pipeline with new ones. This in turn means that, rather than being an on-again, off-again mishmash of projects, your innovation process needs to be carefully orchestrated.

Companies that innovate proficiently manage the process in similar ways. They have a governance structure suitable for innovation: They set aside a separate budget and staff for innovation and allow senior leaders to make go or no-go decisions about it outside the planning processes for individual businesses. The earmarked innovation budget, which gets allocated across projects, means that new initiatives don't have to compete with established businesses for resources. Such companies also have a strong sense of how innovations fit into the larger portfolio, and a line of sight to initiatives in all different stages. They hunt systematically for opportunities, usually searching beyond the boundaries of the firm and its R&D department and figuring out what customers are trying to accomplish and how the firm can help them do it.

8. Experiment, iterate, learn

As I've said for many years, a big mistake companies make all the time is planning new ventures with the same approaches they use for more-established businesses. Instead, they need to focus on experimentation and learning, and be prepared to make a shift or change emphasis as new discoveries happen. The discovery phase is followed by business model definition and incubation, in which a project takes the shape of an actual business and may begin pilot tests or serving customers. Only once the initiative is relatively stable and healthy is it ramped up. All too often, in their haste to get commercial traction, companies rush through this phase; as a result, whatever product they introduce has critical flaws. They also spend way too much money before testing the critical assumptions that will spell success or failure.

Leadership as Orchestration

No leader could cognitively handle the complexity of scores of individual arenas, all at slightly different stages of development. What great leaders do is figure out some key directional guidelines, put in place good processes for core activities such as innovation, and use their influence over a few crucial inflection points to direct the flow of activities in the organization. This requires a new kind of leader—one who initiates conversations that question, rather than reinforce, the status quo. A strong leader seeks contrasting opinions and honest disagreement. Diversity increasingly becomes a tool for picking up signals that things may be changing. Broader constituencies may well become involved in the strategy process.

Finally, transient-advantage leaders recognize the need for speed. Fast and roughly right decision making will replace deliberations that are precise but slow. In a world where advantages last for five minutes, you can blink and miss the window of opportunity.

One thing about strategy hasn't changed: It still requires making tough choices about what to do and, even more important, what not to do. Even though you are orchestrating scores of arenas, you can do only so many things. So defining where you want to compete, how you intend to win, and how you are going to move from advantage to advantage is critical. While we might be tempted to throw up our hands and say that strategy is no longer useful, I think the opposite conclusion is called for. It's more important than ever. It just isn't about the status quo any longer.

Originally published in June 2013. Reprint R1306C

Is Your Company Prepared for the Transient-Advantage Economy?

TO SEIZE TRANSIENT ADVANTAGES, companies need a new mode of operation. The diagnostic below can help pinpoint areas where change is required. Simply position your organization's current way of working between the two statements in the assessment. If you score in the lower part of the range in an area, you might want to take a hard look at it.

Focused on extending existing advantages	1	2	3	4	5	6	7	Capable of coping with transient advantage
Budgets, people, and other resources are largely controlled by heads of established businesses.	1	2	3	4	5	6	7	Critical resources are controlled by a separate group that doesn't run businesses.
We tend to extend our established advantages if we can.	1	2	3	4	5	6	7	We tend to move out of an established advantage early, with the goal of moving on to something new.
We don't have a process for disengaging from a business.	1	2	3	4	5	6	7	We have a systematic way of exiting businesses.
Disengagements tend to be painful and difficult.	1	2	3	4	5	6	7	Disengagements are just part of the normal business cycle.
We try to avoid failures, even in uncertain situations.	1	2	3	4	5	6	7	We recognize that failures are unavoidable and try to learn from them.
We budget annually or for even longer.	1	2	3	4	5	6	7	We budget in quick cycles, either quarterly or on a rolling basis.
We like to stick to plans once they are formulated.	1	2	3	4	5	6	7	We are comfortable changing our plans as new information comes in.

We emphasize optimization in our approach to asset utilization.	1	2	3	4	5	6	7	We emphasize flexibility in our approach to asset utilization.
Innovation is an on-again, off-again process.	1	2	3	4	5	6	7	Innovation is an ongoing, systematic core process for us.
It's difficult for us to pull resources from a successful business to fund more uncertain opportunities.	1	2	3	4	5	6	7	It's quite normal for us to pull resources from a successful business to fund more uncertain opportunities.
Our best people spend most of their time solving problems and handling crises.	1	2	3	4	5	6	7	Our best people spend most of their time working on new opportunities for our organization.
We try to keep our organizational structure relatively stable and to fit new ideas into the existing structure.	1	2	3	4	5	6	7	We reorganize when new opportunities require a different structure.
We tend to emphasize analysis over experimentation.	1	2	3	4	5	6	7	We tend to emphasize experimentation over analysis.
It isn't easy to be candid with our senior leaders when something goes wrong.	1	2	3	4	5	6	7	We find it very easy to be candid with senior leaders when something goes wrong.

Bringing Science to the Art of Strategy

by A.G. Lafley, Roger L. Martin, Jan W. Rivkin, and Nicolaj Siggelkow

STRATEGIC PLANNERS PRIDE THEMSELVES on their rigor. Strategies are supposed to be driven by numbers and extensive analysis and uncontaminated by bias, judgment, or opinion. The larger the spreadsheets, the more confident an organization is in its process. All those numbers, all those analyses, *feel* scientific, and in the modern world, "scientific" equals "good."

Yet if that's the case, why do the operations managers in most large and midsize firms dread the annual strategic planning ritual? Why does it consume so much time and have so little impact on company actions? Talk to those managers, and you will most likely uncover a deeper frustration: the sense that strategic planning does not produce novel strategies. Instead, it perpetuates the status quo.

One common reaction is to become explicitly antiscientific—to throw off the shackles of organized number crunching and resort to off-site "ideation events" or online "jam sessions" intended to promote "out of the box" thinking. These processes may result in radical new ideas, but more likely than not, those ideas cannot be translated into strategic choices that guide productive action. As one manager put it, "There's a reason we keep those ideas outside the box."

Many managers feel they are doomed to weigh the futile rigor of ordinary strategic planning processes against the hit-or-miss creativity of the alternatives. We believe the two can be reconciled to produce creative but realistic strategies. The key is to recognize that *conventional strategic planning is not actually scientific*. Yes, the scientific method is marked by rigorous analysis, and conventional strategic planning has plenty of that. But also integral to the scientific method are the creation of novel hypotheses and the careful generation of custom-tailored tests of those hypotheses—two elements that conventional strategic planning typically lacks. It is as though modern strategic planning decided to be scientific but then chopped off essential elements of science.

The approach we're about to describe adapts the scientific method to the needs of business strategy. Triggered by the emergence of a strategic challenge or opportunity, it starts with the formulation of well-articulated hypotheses—what we term *possibilities*. It then asks what would have to be true about the world for each possibility to be supported. Only then does it unleash analysts to determine which of the possibilities is most likely to succeed. In this way, our approach takes the strategy-making process from the merely rigorous (or unrealistically creative) to the truly scientific. (See the sidebar "Seven Steps to Strategy Making.")

Step 1. Move from Issues to Choice

Conventional strategic planning is driven by the calendar and tends to focus on issues, such as declining profits or market share. As long as this is the case, the organization will fall into the trap of investigating data related to the issues rather than exploring and testing possible solutions.

A simple way to get strategists to avoid that trap is to require them to define two mutually exclusive options that could resolve the issue in question. Once you have framed the problem as a choice—any choice—your analysis and emotions will focus on what you have to do next, not on describing or analyzing the challenge. The possibilities-based approach therefore begins with the recognition that the organization must make a choice and that the choice has consequences. For the management team, this is

Idea in Brief

For all its emphasis on data and number crunching, conventional strategic planning is not actually scientific. It lacks the genuine inquiry that's at the heart of the scientific method.

To produce novel strategies, teams need to adopt a step-by-step process in which creative thinking yields possibilities and rigorous analysis tests them. They should ask what *must be true* for a given possibility to succeed—and explore whether those conditions hold. The decision is then straightforward: Choose the possibility with the fewest barriers to success.

P&G took this path in the late 1990s, when it sought to become a major global player in skin care. The strategy it arrived at—reinventing Olay as an upscale product also sold in mass channels—succeeded beyond expectations. This shows what can happen when teams shift their focus from "What is the right answer?" to "What are the right questions?"

the proverbial crossing of the Rubicon—the step that starts the strategy-making process.

In the late 1990s, when Procter & Gamble was contemplating becoming a major player in the global beauty care sector, it had a big issue: It lacked a credible brand in skin care, the largest and most profitable segment of the sector. All it had was Oil of Olay, a small, down-market brand with an aging consumer base. P&G crossed its Rubicon and laid out two possibilities: It could attempt to dramatically transform Oil of Olay into a worthy competitor of brands like L'Oréal, Clarins, and La Prairie, or it could spend billions of dollars to buy a major existing skin care brand. This framing helped managers internalize the magnitude of what was at stake. At that point P&G turned from contemplating an issue to facing a serious choice.

Step 2. Generate Strategic Possibilities

Having recognized that a choice needs to be made, you can now turn to the full range of possibilities you should consider. These might be versions of the options already identified. For example, P&G could try to grow Oil of Olay in its current price tier or take it upmarket, or it could seek to buy the German company that owns Nivea or pry

Seven Steps to Strategy Making

APPLYING CREATIVITY to a scientifically rigorous process enables teams to generate novel strategies and to pinpoint the one most likely to succeed.

1. **Frame a choice.** Convert your issue into at least two mutually exclusive options that might resolve it.

2. **Generate possibilities.** Broaden your list of options to ensure an inclusive range of possibilities.

3. **Specify conditions.** For each possibility, describe what must be true for it to be strategically sound.

4. **Identify barriers.** Determine which conditions are least likely to hold true.

5. **Design tests.** For each key barrier condition, devise a test you deem valid and sufficient to generate commitment.

6. **Conduct the tests.** Start with the tests for the barrier conditions in which you have the least confidence.

7. **Make your choice.** Review your key conditions in light of your test results in order to reach a decision.

Clinique out of the hands of Estée Lauder. Possibilities might also exist outside the initial options. For instance, P&G could extend its successful cosmetics brand, Cover Girl, into skin care and build a global brand on that platform.

Constructing strategic possibilities, especially ones that are genuinely new, is the ultimate creative act in business. No one in the rest of the beauty industry would have imagined P&G's completely reinventing Olay and boldly going head-to-head against leading prestige brands. To generate such creative options, you need a clear idea of what constitutes a possibility. You also need an imaginative yet grounded team and a robust process for managing debate.

Desired output

A possibility is essentially a happy story that describes how a firm might succeed. Each story lays out where the company plays in its market and how it wins there. It should have internally consistent logic, but it need not be proved at this point. As long as we can imagine that it *could* be valid, it makes the cut. Characterizing possibilities as stories that do not require proof helps people discuss what might be viable but does not yet exist. It is much easier to tell a story about why a possibility could make sense than to provide data on the odds that it will succeed.

A common temptation is to sketch out possibilities only at the highest level. But a motto ("Go global") or a goal ("Be number one") does not constitute a strategic possibility. We push teams to specify in detail the *advantage* they aim to achieve or leverage, the *scope* across which the advantage applies, and the *activities* throughout the value chain that would deliver the intended advantage across the targeted scope. Otherwise it is impossible to unpack the logic underlying a possibility and to subject the possibility to subsequent tests. In the Cover Girl possibility, the advantage would come from Cover Girl's strong brand and existing consumer base combined with Procter & Gamble's R&D and global go-to-market capabilities. The scope would be limited to the younger demographic at the heart of the current Cover Girl consumer base, and it would need to build internationally from North America, where the brand was strong. The key activities would include leveraging Cover Girl's stable of model and celebrity endorsers.

Managers often ask, "How many possibilities should we generate?" The answer varies according to context. Some industries offer few happy stories—there are simply not a lot of good alternatives. Others, particularly ones in ferment or with numerous customer segments, have many potential directions. We find that most teams consider three to five possibilities in depth. On one aspect of this question we are adamant: The team *must* produce more than one possibility. Otherwise it never really started the strategy-making process, because it didn't see itself as facing a choice. Analyzing a single possibility is not conducive to producing optimal action—or, in fact, any action at all.

We also insist that the status quo or current trajectory be among the possibilities considered. This forces the team in later stages to specify what must be true for the status quo to be viable, thereby eliminating the common implicit assumption "Worst case, we can just keep doing what we're already doing." The status quo is some-times a path to decline. By including it among the possibilities, a team makes it subject to investigation and potential doubt.

The team at P&G surfaced five strategic possibilities in addition to the status quo. One was to abandon Oil of Olay and acquire a major global skin care brand. A second was to keep Oil of Olay posi-tioned where it was, as an entry-priced, mass-market brand, and to strengthen its appeal to current older consumers by leveraging R&D capabilities to improve its wrinkle-reduction performance. A third was to take Oil of Olay into the prestige distribution channel—department stores and specialty beauty shops—as an upscale brand. A fourth was to completely reinvent Olay as a prestigelike brand that would appeal more broadly to younger women (age 35 to 50) but be sold in traditional mass channels by retail partners willing to create a "masstige" experience, with a special display section. A fifth was to extend the Cover Girl brand to skin care.

The people

The group tasked with dreaming up strategic possibilities should represent a diversity of specialties, backgrounds, and experiences. Otherwise it is difficult to generate creative possibilities and to flesh out each one in sufficient detail. We find it useful to include individuals who did not create, and therefore are not emotionally bound to, the status quo. This usually implies that promising junior execu-tives will participate. We also find that individuals from outside the firm, preferably outside the industry, often lend the most original ideas. Finally, we believe it's crucial to include operations manag-ers, not just staff members, in the process. This not only deepens practical wisdom but also builds early commitment to and knowl-edge of the strategy that is ultimately chosen. If you show us a com-pany where the planners are different from the doers, we will show you a company where what gets done is different from what was planned.

Optimal group size varies among organizations and their cul-tures. Companies with a culture of inclusion, for example, should assemble a large group. If you go this route, use breakout groups to discuss the specific possibilities; a group larger than eight or 10 people tends to be self-censoring.

It's usually not a good idea to have the most senior person serve as the leader; she will have a difficult time convincing the others that she is not playing her usual role as boss. Instead, choose a respected lower-level insider who is not perceived as having a strong point of view on which course should be chosen. Or tap an outside facilitator who has some experience with the firm.

The rules

Once selected, the possibility generators must commit themselves to separating their first step—the creation of possibilities—from the subsequent steps of testing and selecting. Managers with critical minds naturally tend to greet each new idea with a long list of reasons why it won't work. The leader must constantly remind the group that ample time for skepticism will come later; for now, it must suspend judgment. If anyone persists with a critique, the leader should require him to reframe it as a condition and table it for discussion in the next step. For example, the critique "Customers will never accept differential pricing" becomes the condition "This possibility requires that customers accept differential pricing." It's particularly important that the leader not shoot down possibilities early. If that happens, it's open season on all possibilities. And removing an option about which a particular team member feels strongly may cause that person to withdraw from the process.

Many management teams try to generate strategic possibilities in a single off-site brainstorming session. Such sessions are useful, especially if they are held at an unusual location that gets people out of their accustomed routines and habits of mind. But we have also seen teams benefit from spreading the possibility-generation process over some time so that individuals have an opportunity to reflect, think creatively, and build on ideas. It is perhaps most effective to start by asking each person to spend 30 to 45 minutes sketching out three to five (or more) stories. The stories do not need to be detailed; they should truly be sketches. After this exercise the group (or breakout groups) fleshes out the initial possibilities.

Possibility generation centers on creativity, and many techniques purport to boost creativity. We've found three kinds of probing questions to be especially useful. *Inside-out* questions start with the company's assets and capabilities and then reason outward: What does this company do especially well that parts of the market might value and that might produce a superior wedge between buyer value and costs? *Outside-in* questions look for openings in the market: What are the underserved needs, what are the needs that customers find hard to express, and what gaps have competitors left? *Far-outside-in* questions use analogical reasoning: What would it take to be the Google, the Apple, or the Walmart of this market?

You will know that you have a good set of possibilities for further work if two things prove to be true. First, the status quo doesn't look like a brilliant idea: At least one other possibility intrigues the group enough to make it really question the existing order. Second, at least one possibility makes most of the group uncomfortable: It is sufficiently far from the status quo that the group questions whether it would be at all doable or safe. If one or both of these don't hold, it is probably time for another round of possibility generation.

The uncomfortable possibility for P&G was the fourth option described above. It involved transforming a weak, low-end brand into a more desirable player that could compete with upmarket department store products and then creating an entirely new masstige segment that mass retailers would enthusiastically support.

Step 3. Specify the Conditions for Success

The purpose of this step is to specify what *must be true* for each possibility to be a terrific choice. Note that this step is not intended for arguing about what *is* true. It is not intended to explore or assess the soundness of the logic behind the various possibilities or to consider data that may or may not support the logic—that comes later. Any consideration of evidence at this point detracts from the process.

The importance of this distinction cannot be overstated. When the discussion of a possibility centers on *what is true,* the person most skeptical about the possibility attacks it vigorously, hoping to knock it out of contention. The originator defends it, parrying arguments in order to protect its viability. Tempers rise, statements become more extreme, and relationships are strained. Meanwhile, little of either opponent's logic is revealed to the other.

If, instead, the dialogue is about *what would have to be true,* then the skeptic can say, "For me to be confident in this possibility, I would have to know that consumers will embrace this sort of offering." That is a very different sort of statement from "That will never work!" It helps the proponent understand the skeptic's reservations and develop the proof to overcome them. It also makes the skeptic specify the exact source of the skepticism rather than issue a blanket denunciation.

We've developed a framework for surfacing the conditions that have to be true for a possibility to be an attractive strategy (see the sidebar "Assessing the Validity of a Strategic Option"). The conditions fall into seven categories relating to the industry, customer value, business model, and competitors. Begin by clearly spelling out the strategic possibility under consideration. Then move to a two-stage discussion process:

Generate a list

In the first stage of discussion, the aim is to enumerate all the conditions that need to hold true for everyone in the room to be able to honestly say, "I feel confident enough to make this possibility a reality." The conditions should be expressed as declarative rather than conditional statements—for example, "Channel partners will support us," not "Channel partners would have to support us." This helps paint a positive picture of the possibility, one that will be inviting to the group if the conditions actually hold.

You must make sure that the individual who proposed the possibility under review does not dominate this conversation. Any condition that is put forward should be added to the list. The person putting it forward should simply be asked to explain why that condition would be necessary for him to be confident; he should not be challenged about the truth of the condition.

Assessing the Validity of a Strategic Option

ONCE YOU'VE LISTED ALL YOUR OPTIONS, specify what must be true for each to succeed. The diagram below provides a framework for surfacing the necessary conditions; in effect, you are reverse engineering your choice. P&G's application of the framework to its option for a renamed and repositioned Olay is shown on the next page.

The framework

In order to pursue this option successfully, what conditions would we have to believe existed or could be created?

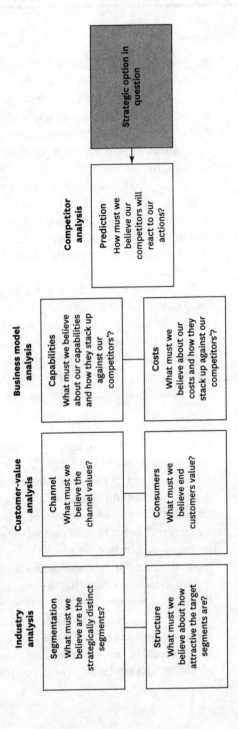

Industry analysis

Segmentation
What must we believe are the strategically distinct segments?

Structure
What must we believe about how attractive the target segments are?

Customer-value analysis

Channel
What must we believe the channel values?

Consumers
What must we believe end customers value?

Business model analysis

Capabilities
What must we believe about our capabilities and how they stack up against our competitors'?

Costs
What must we believe about our costs and how they stack up against our competitors'?

Competitor analysis

Prediction
How must we believe our competitors will react to our actions?

Strategic option in question

The Olay "masstige" option

The option under consideration was to reposition Olay for a younger demographic, with the promise to "fight the seven signs of aging."
It would involve partnering with retailers to create a masstige segment—consumers willing to buy a prestigelike product in mass channels.
P&G determined that for this option to succeed, these conditions would have to exist or be created:

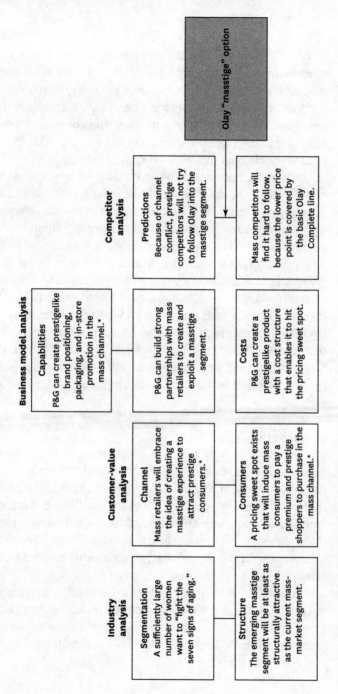

Industry analysis

Segmentation
A sufficiently large number of women want to "fight the seven signs of aging."

Structure
The emerging masstige segment will be at least as structurally attractive as the current mass-market segment.

Customer-value analysis

Channel
Mass retailers will embrace the idea of creating a masstige experience to attract prestige consumers.*

Consumers
A pricing sweet spot exists that will induce mass consumers to pay a premium and prestige shoppers to purchase in the mass channel.*

Business model analysis

Capabilities
P&G can create prestigelike brand positioning, packaging, and in-store promotion in the mass channel.*

P&G can build strong partnerships with mass retailers to create and exploit a masstige segment.

Costs
P&G can create a prestigelike product with a cost structure that enables it to hit the pricing sweet spot.

Competitor analysis

Predictions
Because of channel conflict, prestige competitors will not try to follow Olay into the masstige segment.

Mass competitors will find it hard to follow, because the lower price point is covered by the basic Olay Complete line.

Olay "masstige" option

*Barrier conditions: The ones P&G thought least likely to hold true

When each member of the group has had a chance to add conditions to the list, the facilitator should read the list aloud and ask the group, "If all these conditions were true, would you advocate for and support this choice?" If everyone says yes, it's time to move to the next step. If any members say no, they must be asked, "What additional condition would enable you to answer yes?" This line of questioning should continue until every member replies affirmatively.

Once again, during this step expressing opinions about whether or not conditions are true should be strictly prohibited. The point is simply to ferret out *what would have to be true* for every member of the group to feel cognitively and emotionally committed to each possibility under consideration.

It is important to treat the current strategy in this way as well. We recall one discussion a number of years ago about the status quo option. Toward the end, the president of the company leaped out of his seat and sprinted from the room. When he returned, 10 minutes later, his colleagues asked whether he was OK. He explained that the discussion had made him see how logically weak the status quo was. The reason he had raced out was to cancel a multimillion-dollar initiative in support of the status quo—the go/no-go deadline was that very day.

Weed the list

The previous exercise typically overshoots, and the list of conditions crosses the line between "must have" and "nice to have." After finishing the list of conditions, the group should take a break and then review the items, asking, "If every condition but this one held true, would you eliminate the possibility or still view it as viable?" If the answer is the former, the condition is a must-have and should be maintained. If it is the latter, it is a nice-to-have and should be removed.

The goal here is to ensure that the list of conditions is truly a binding set. To this end, once you're finished reviewing, you should ask, "If all these conditions were true, would you advocate for and support this choice?" If any member says no, then the group needs to return to the first-stage discussion and add any necessary conditions that were initially overlooked or mistakenly removed.

After arriving at a full set of possibilities and ensuring that all must-have conditions are attached to each, the group needs to bring its options to the executives whose approval will be required to ratify the final choice and to any other colleagues who might stand in the way. For each possibility, the group needs to ask these people the same questions it asked its members: "If these conditions were shown to hold true, would you choose this possibility? If not, what additional conditions would you include?" The goal is to make sure that the conditions for each possibility are well specified in the eyes of everyone with a say in the choice—*before* analysis ensues.

Step 4. Identify the Barriers to Choice

Now it's time to cast a critical eye on the conditions. The task is to assess which ones you believe are least likely to hold true. They will define the barriers to choosing that possibility.

Begin by asking group members to imagine that they could buy a guarantee that any particular condition will hold true. To which condition would they apply it? The condition they choose is, by inference, the biggest barrier to choosing the possibility under consideration. The next condition to which they would apply a guarantee is the next-biggest barrier, and so on. The ideal output is an ordered list of barriers to each possibility, two or three of which really worry the group. If there is disagreement about the ordering of particular conditions, you should rank them as equal.

Pay close attention to the member who is most skeptical that a given condition will hold true; that person represents the greatest obstacle—and, in the case of a problematic possibility, an extremely valuable obstacle—to the selection and pursuit of the option. Members must be encouraged to raise, not suppress, their concerns. Even if only one person is concerned about a given condition, the condition must be kept on the list. Otherwise he would be within his rights to dismiss the final analysis. If the skepticism of every member is drawn out and taken seriously, all will feel confident in the process and the outcomes.

When the P&G beauty care team reviewed the nine conditions it had come up with for the Olay masstige possibility, the members felt confident that six would hold: The potential consumer segment was big enough to be worth targeting; the segment was at least as structurally attractive as the current mass-market skin care segment; P&G could produce the product at a cost that would permit a somewhat lower price than those of key lower-end prestige players; it was capable of building retailer partnerships (if retailers liked the idea); prestige competitors would not copy the strategy; and mass competitors could not copy the strategy. However, three conditions worried the team, in descending order: that mass-channel consumers would accept a new, significantly higher starting price point; that mass-channel players would be game to create a new masstige segment; and that P&G could bring together prestigelike brand positioning, product packaging, and in-store promotion elements in the mass-retail channel.

Step 5. Design Tests for the Barrier Conditions

Once you've identified and ordered the key barrier conditions, the group must test each one to see whether it holds true. The test might involve surveying a thousand customers or speaking to a single supplier. It might entail crunching thousands of numbers or avoiding any quantifiers at all. The only requirement is that the entire group believe that the test is valid and can form the basis for rejecting the possibility in question or generating commitment to it.

The member who is most skeptical about a given condition should take the lead in designing and applying the test for it. This person will typically have the highest standard of proof; if she is satisfied that the condition has passed the test, everyone else will be satisfied. The risk, of course, is that the skeptic might set an unachievable standard. In practice this does not happen, for two reasons. First, people demonstrate extreme skepticism largely because they don't feel heard. In a typical buy-in process, concerns are treated as roadblocks to be pushed aside as quickly as is feasible. The possibilities-based approach ensures that individuals with concerns both feel and actually are heard. Second is the specter of mutually assured destruction. Though I may have serious doubts about possibility A, I quite like possibility B. You, on the other hand, have few doubts about possibility A but have serious qualms about choosing possibility B. I get to set the tests for the barrier conditions for possibility A, but I do so with the knowledge that you will be setting the tests for possibility B. If I set too high a bar, you will surely do the same. Being fair and sensible is, then, the smartest approach.

Step 6. Conduct the Tests

We typically structure this step according to what we call "the lazy man's approach to choice," testing conditions in the reverse order of the group's confidence. That is, the condition the group feels is least likely to hold up is tested first. If the group's suspicion is right, the possibility at hand can be eliminated without any further testing. If that condition passes the test, the condition with the next-lowest likelihood of confirmation is tested, and so on. Because testing is often the most expensive and time-consuming part of the process, the lazy man's approach can save enormous resources.

Typically, at this step you bring in people from outside the strategy team—consultants or experts in relevant functional or geographic units, who can help fine-tune and conduct the tests you have prioritized. It is important to ensure that they concentrate solely on testing. You are not asking them to revisit the conditions. In fact, one beauty of the possibilities-based approach is that it enables you to focus outside resources that may be costly and time-consuming.

This approach differs profoundly from the process followed by most strategy consultants, who conduct a relatively standard suite of analyses in parallel. That generates a lot of (expensive) analysis, much of which turns out to be not essential or even useful in decision making. Furthermore, depth is sacrificed for breadth: Analyses are a mile wide and an inch deep, because the cost of deep analysis across the board would be prohibitive. To generate choice and commitment, we need analysis that is an inch wide and a mile deep—targeting the concerns that could prevent the group from choosing an option and exploring those areas thoroughly enough to meet the group's standard of proof. The possibilities-based approach permits this.

For the P&G beauty care team, the most challenging condition for the Olay masstige possibility related to pricing. The test of the condition showcased the ability of a truly scientific, hypothesis-driven approach to generate strategies that are both unexpected and successful. Joe Listro, Olay's R&D manager, explains how it went. "We started to test the new Olay product at premium price points of $12.99 to $18.99 and got very different results," he says. "At $12.99, there was a positive response and a reasonably good rate of purchase intent. But most who signaled a desire to buy at $12.99 were mass shoppers. Very few department store shoppers were interested at that price point. Basically, we were trading people up from within the channel. At $15.99, purchase intent dropped dramatically. At $18.99, it went back up again—way up. So $12.99 was really good, $15.99 not so good, $18.99 great."

The team learned that at $18.99, consumers were crossing over from prestige department and specialty stores to buy Olay in discount, drug, and grocery stores. That price point sent exactly the right message. For the department store shopper, the product was a great value but still credibly expensive. For the mass shopper, the premium price signified that the product must be considerably better than anything else on the shelf. In contrast, $15.99 was in no-man's land—for a mass shopper, expensive without signaling differentiation, and for a prestige shopper, not expensive enough. These differences were quite fine; had the team not focused so carefully on building and applying robust tests for multiple price points, the findings might never have emerged.

It is important to understand that tests cannot eliminate all uncertainty. Even the best-performing possibility will entail some risk. That is why it is so crucial to set testable conditions for the status quo: The team then clearly sees that the status quo is not free of risk. Rather than compare the best-performing possibility with a nonexistent risk-free option, the team can compare the risk of the leading option with the risk of the status quo and reach a decision in that context.

Step 7. Make the Choice

In traditional strategy making, finally choosing a strategy can be difficult and acrimonious. The decision makers usually go off-site and try to frame their binders of much-discussed market research as strategic options. With the stakes high and the logic for each option never clearly articulated, such meetings often end up as negotiations between powerful executives with strong preconceptions. And once the meetings are concluded, those who are skeptical of the decision begin to undermine it.

With the possibilities-based approach, the choice-making step becomes simple, even anticlimactic. The group needs only to review the analytical test results and choose the possibility that faces the fewest serious barriers.

Often a strategy chosen in this way is surprisingly bold and would most likely have been strangled at birth in the traditional process. Consider the Olay case. P&G ended up deciding to launch an upmarket product called Olay Total Effects for $18.99. In other words, the brand once dismissed as "Oil for Old Ladies" was transformed into a prestigelike product line at a price point close to that of department store brands. And it worked. Mass-retail partners loved the product and saw new shoppers buying at new price points in their stores. Beauty magazine editors and dermatologists saw real value in the well-priced, effective product line.

The masstige strategy succeeded beyond expectations. P&G would have been happy with a billion-dollar global skin care brand. But in less than a decade the Olay brand surpassed $2.5 billion in annual sales by spawning a series of "boutique" product lines—starting with Total Effects and following with Regenerist, Definity, and Pro-X—that attracted more prestige shoppers and commanded prices eventually exceeding $50.

Laid out neatly on paper, the possibilities-based approach sounds easy. But many managers struggle with it—not because the mechanics are hard, but because the approach requires at least three fundamental shifts in mind-set. First, in the early steps, they must avoid asking "What should we do?" and instead ask "What might we do?" Managers, especially those who pride themselves on being decisive, jump naturally to the former question and get restless when tackling the latter.

Second, in the middle steps, managers must shift from asking "What do I believe?" to asking "What would I have to believe?" This requires a manager to imagine that each possibility, including ones he does not like, is a great idea, and such a mind-set does not come naturally to most people. It's needed, however, to identify the right tests for a possibility.

Finally, by focusing a team on pinpointing the critical conditions and tests, the possibilities-based approach forces managers to move away from asking "What is the right answer?" and concentrate instead on "What are the right questions? What specifically must we know in order to make a good decision?" In our experience, most managers are better at advocacy of their own views than at inquiry, especially about others' views. The possibilities-based approach relies on and fosters a team's ability to inquire. And genuine inquiry must lie at the heart of any process that aims to be scientific.

Originally published in September 2012. **Reprint** R1209C

Managing Risks

A New Framework. *by Robert S. Kaplan and Anette Mikes*

WHEN TONY HAYWARD BECAME CEO OF BP, in 2007, he vowed to make safety his top priority. Among the new rules he instituted were the requirements that all employees use lids on coffee cups while walking and refrain from texting while driving. Three years later, on Hayward's watch, the *Deepwater Horizon* oil rig exploded in the Gulf of Mexico, causing one of the worst man-made disasters in history. A U.S. investigation commission attributed the disaster to management failures that crippled "the ability of individuals involved to identify the risks they faced and to properly evaluate, communicate, and address them."

Hayward's story reflects a common problem. Despite all the rhetoric and money invested in it, risk management is too often treated as a compliance issue that can be solved by drawing up lots of rules and making sure that all employees follow them. Many such rules, of course, are sensible and do reduce some risks that could severely damage a company. But rules-based risk management will not diminish either the likelihood or the impact of a disaster such as Deepwater Horizon, just as it did not prevent the failure of many financial institutions during the 2007–2008 credit crisis.

Understanding the three categories of risk

The risks that companies face fall into three categories, each of which requires a different risk-management approach. Preventable risks, arising from within an organization, are monitored and controlled through rules, values, and standard compliance tools. In contrast, strategy risks and external risks require distinct processes that encourage managers to openly discuss risks and find cost-effective ways to reduce the likelihood of risk events or mitigate their consequences.

Category 1: Preventable risks	Category 2: Strategy risks	Category 3: External risks
Risks arising from within the company that generate no strategic benefits	Risks taken for superior strategic returns	External, uncontrollable risks
Risk mitigation objective		
Avoid or eliminate occurrence cost-effectively	Reduce likelihood and impact cost-effectively	Reduce impact cost-effectively should a risk event occur
Control model		
Integrated culture-and-compliance model: Develop mission statement; values and belief systems; rules and boundary systems; standard operating procedures; internal controls and internal audit	Interactive discussions about risks to strategic objectives drawing on tools such as: • Maps of likelihood and impact of identified risks • Key risk indicator (KRI) scorecards Resource allocation to mitigate critical risk events	"Envisioning" risks through: • Tail-risk assessments and stress testing • Scenario planning • War-gaming
Role of risk-management staff function		
Coordinates, oversees, and revises specific risk controls with internal audit function	Runs risk workshops and risk review meetings Helps develop portfolio of risk initiatives and their funding Acts as devil's advocates	Runs stress-testing, scenario-planning, and war-gaming exercises with management team Acts as devil's advocates
Relationship of the risk-management function to business units		
Acts as independent overseers	Acts as independent facilitators, independent experts, or embedded experts	Complements strategy team or serves as independent facilitators of "envisioning" exercises

Idea in Brief

For all the rhetoric about its importance and the money invested in it, risk management is too often treated as a compliance issue.

A rules-based risk-management system may work well to align values and control employee behavior, but it is unsuitable for managing risks inherent in a company's strategic choices or the risks posed by major disruptions or changes in the external environment. Those types of risk require systems aimed at generating discussion and debate.

For strategy risks, companies must tailor approaches to the scope of the risks involved and their rate of change. Though the risk-management functions may vary from company to company, all such efforts must be anchored in corporate strategic-planning processes.

To manage major external risks outside the company's control, companies can call on tools such as war-gaming and scenario analysis. The choice of approach depends on the immediacy of the potential risk's impact and whether it arises from geopolitical, environmental, economic, or competitive changes.

In this article, we present a new categorization of risk that allows executives to tell which risks can be managed through a rules-based model and which require alternative approaches. We examine the individual and organizational challenges inherent in generating open, constructive discussions about managing the risks related to strategic choices and argue that companies need to anchor these discussions in their strategy formulation and implementation processes. We conclude by looking at how organizations can identify and prepare for nonpreventable risks that arise externally to their strategy and operations.

Managing Risk: Rules or Dialogue?

The first step in creating an effective risk-management system is to understand the qualitative distinctions among the types of risks that organizations face. Our field research shows that risks fall into one of three categories. Risk events from any category can be fatal to a company's strategy and even to its survival.

Identifying and Managing Preventable Risks

COMPANIES CANNOT ANTICIPATE EVERY CIRCUMSTANCE or conflict of interest that an employee might encounter.

Thus, the first line of defense against preventable risk events is to provide guidelines clarifying the company's goals and values.

The Mission

A well-crafted mission statement articulates the organization's fundamental purpose, serving as a "true north" for all employees to follow. The first sentence of Johnson & Johnson's renowned credo, for instance, states, "We believe our first responsibility is to the doctors, nurses and patients, to mothers and fathers, and all others who use our products and services," making clear to all employees whose interests should take precedence in any situation. Mission statements should be communicated to and understood by all employees.

The Values

Companies should articulate the values that guide employee behavior toward principal stakeholders, including customers, suppliers, fellow employees, communities, and shareholders. Clear value statements help employees avoid violating the company's standards and putting its reputation and assets at risk.

Category I: Preventable risks

These are internal risks, arising from within the organization, that are controllable and ought to be eliminated or avoided. Examples are the risks from employees' and managers' unauthorized, illegal, unethical, incorrect, or inappropriate actions and the risks from breakdowns in routine operational processes. To be sure, companies should have a zone of tolerance for defects or errors that would not cause severe damage to the enterprise and for which achieving complete avoidance would be too costly. But in general, companies should seek to eliminate these risks since they get no strategic benefits from taking them on. A rogue trader or an employee bribing a local official may produce some short-term profits for the firm, but over time such actions will diminish the company's value.

The Boundaries

A strong corporate culture clarifies what is not allowed. An explicit definition of boundaries is an effective way to control actions. Consider that nine of the Ten Commandments and nine of the first 10 amendments to the U.S. Constitution (commonly known as the Bill of Rights) are written in negative terms. Companies need corporate codes of business conduct that prescribe behaviors relating to conflicts of interest, antitrust issues, trade secrets and confidential information, bribery, discrimination, and harassment.

Of course, clearly articulated statements of mission, values, and boundaries don't in themselves ensure good behavior. To counter the day-to-day pressures of organizational life, top managers must serve as role models and demonstrate that they mean what they say. Companies must institute strong internal control systems, such as the segregation of duties and an active whistle-blowing program, to reduce not only misbehavior but also temptation. A capable and independent internal audit department tasked with continually checking employees' compliance with internal controls and standard operating processes also will deter employees from violating company procedures and policies and can detect violations when they do occur.

This risk category is best managed through active prevention: monitoring operational processes and guiding people's behaviors and decisions toward desired norms. Since considerable literature already exists on the rules-based compliance approach, we refer interested readers to the sidebar "Identifying and Managing Preventable Risks" in lieu of a full discussion of best practices here.

Category II: Strategy risks

A company voluntarily accepts some risk in order to generate superior returns from its strategy. A bank assumes credit risk, for example, when it lends money; many companies take on risks through their research and development activities.

Strategy risks are quite different from preventable risks because they are not inherently undesirable. A strategy with high expected returns generally requires the company to take on significant risks, and managing those risks is a key driver in capturing the potential gains. BP accepted the high risks of drilling several miles below the surface of the Gulf of Mexico because of the high value of the oil and gas it hoped to extract.

Strategy risks cannot be managed through a rules-based control model. Instead, you need a risk-management system designed to reduce the probability that the assumed risks actually materialize and to improve the company's ability to manage or contain the risk events should they occur. Such a system would not stop companies from undertaking risky ventures; to the contrary, it would enable companies to take on higher-risk, higher-reward ventures than could competitors with less effective risk management.

Category III: External risks

Some risks arise from events outside the company and are beyond its influence or control. Sources of these risks include natural and political disasters and major macroeconomic shifts. External risks require yet another approach. Because companies cannot prevent such events from occurring, their management must focus on identification (they tend to be obvious in hindsight) and mitigation of their impact.

Companies should tailor their risk-management processes to these different categories. While a compliance-based approach is effective for managing preventable risks, it is wholly inadequate for strategy risks or external risks, which require a fundamentally different approach based on open and explicit risk discussions. That, however, is easier said than done; extensive behavioral and organizational research has shown that individuals have strong cognitive biases that discourage them from thinking about and discussing risk until it's too late.

Why Risk Is Hard to Talk About

Multiple studies have found that people overestimate their ability to influence events that, in fact, are heavily determined by chance. We tend to be *overconfident* about the accuracy of our forecasts and risk assessments and far too narrow in our assessment of the range of outcomes that may occur.

We also *anchor our estimates* to readily available evidence despite the known danger of making linear extrapolations from recent history to a highly uncertain and variable future. We often compound this problem with a *confirmation bias,* which drives us to favor information that supports our positions (typically successes) and suppress information that contradicts them (typically failures). When events depart from our expectations, we tend to *escalate commitment,* irrationally directing even more resources to our failed course of action—throwing good money after bad.

Organizational biases also inhibit our ability to discuss risk and failure. In particular, teams facing uncertain conditions often engage in *groupthink*: Once a course of action has gathered support within a group, those not yet on board tend to suppress their objections—however valid—and fall in line. Groupthink is especially likely if the team is led by an overbearing or overconfident manager who wants to minimize conflict, delay, and challenges to his or her authority.

Collectively, these individual and organizational biases explain why so many companies overlook or misread ambiguous threats. Rather than mitigating risk, firms actually incubate risk through the *normalization of deviance,* as they learn to tolerate apparently minor failures and defects and treat early warning signals as false alarms rather than alerts to imminent danger.

Effective risk-management processes must counteract those biases. "Risk mitigation is painful, not a natural act for humans to perform," says Gentry Lee, the chief systems engineer at Jet Propulsion Laboratory (JPL), a division of the U.S. National Aeronautics and Space Administration. The rocket scientists on JPL project teams are top graduates from elite universities, many of whom have never experienced failure at school or work. Lee's biggest challenge in establishing a new risk culture at JPL was to get project teams to feel comfortable thinking and talking about what could go wrong with their excellent designs.

Rules about what to do and what not to do won't help here. In fact, they usually have the opposite effect, encouraging a checklist mentality that inhibits challenge and discussion. Managing strategy risks and external risks requires very different approaches. We start by examining how to identify and mitigate strategy risks.

Managing Strategy Risks

Over the past 10 years of study, we've come across three distinct approaches to managing strategy risks. Which model is appropriate for a given firm depends largely on the context in which an organization operates. Each approach requires quite different structures and roles for a risk-management function, but all three encourage employees to challenge existing assumptions and debate risk information. Our finding that "one size does not fit all" runs counter to the efforts of regulatory authorities and professional associations to standardize the function.

Independent experts

Some organizations—particularly those like JPL that push the envelope of technological innovation—face high intrinsic risk as they pursue long, complex, and expensive product-development projects. But since much of the risk arises from coping with known laws of nature, the risk changes slowly over time. For these organizations, risk management can be handled at the project level.

JPL, for example, has established a risk review board made up of independent technical experts whose role is to challenge project engineers' design, risk-assessment, and risk-mitigation decisions. The experts ensure that evaluations of risk take place periodically throughout the product-development cycle. Because the risks are relatively unchanging, the review board needs to meet only once or twice a year, with the project leader and the head of the review board meeting quarterly.

The risk review board meetings are intense, creating what Gentry Lee calls "a culture of intellectual confrontation." As board member Chris Lewicki says, "We tear each other apart, throwing stones and giving very critical commentary about everything that's going on." In the process, project engineers see their work from another perspective. "It lifts their noses away from the grindstone," Lewicki adds.

The meetings, both constructive and confrontational, are not intended to inhibit the project team from pursuing highly ambitious missions and designs. But they force engineers to think in advance about how they will describe and defend their design decisions and whether they have sufficiently considered likely failures and defects. The board members, acting as devil's advocates, counterbalance the engineers' natural overconfidence, helping to avoid escalation of commitment to projects with unacceptable levels of risk.

At JPL, the risk review board not only promotes vigorous debate about project risks but also has authority over budgets. The board establishes cost and time reserves to be set aside for each project component according to its degree of innovativeness. A simple extension from a prior mission would require a 10% to 20% financial reserve, for instance, whereas an entirely new component that had yet to work on Earth—much less on an unexplored planet—could require a 50% to 75% contingency. The reserves ensure that when problems inevitably arise, the project team has access to the money and time needed to resolve them without jeopardizing the launch date. JPL takes the estimates seriously; projects have been deferred or canceled if funds were insufficient to cover recommended reserves.

Facilitators

Many organizations, such as traditional energy and water utilities, operate in stable technological and market environments, with relatively predictable customer demand. In these situations risks stem largely from seemingly unrelated operational choices across a complex organization that accumulate gradually and can remain hidden for a long time.

Since no single staff group has the knowledge to perform operational-level risk management across diverse functions, firms may deploy a relatively small central risk-management group that collects information from operating managers. This increases managers' awareness of the risks that have been taken on across the organization and provides decision makers with a full picture of the company's risk profile.

We observed this model in action at Hydro One, the Canadian electricity company. Chief risk officer John Fraser, with the explicit backing of the CEO, runs dozens of workshops each year at which employees from all levels and functions identify and rank the principal risks they see to the company's strategic objectives. Employees use an anonymous voting technology to rate each risk, on a scale of 1 to 5, in terms of its impact, the likelihood of occurrence, and the strength of existing controls. The rankings are discussed in the workshops, and employees are empowered to voice and debate their risk perceptions. The group ultimately develops a consensus view that gets recorded on a visual risk map, recommends action plans, and designates an "owner" for each major risk.

Hydro One strengthens accountability by linking capital allocation and budgeting decisions to identified risks. The corporate-level capital-planning process allocates hundreds of millions of dollars, principally to projects that reduce risk effectively and efficiently. The risk group draws upon technical experts to challenge line engineers' investment plans and risk assessments and to provide independent expert oversight to the resource allocation process. At the annual capital allocation meeting, line managers have to defend their proposals in front of their peers and top executives. Managers want their projects to attract funding in the risk-based capital planning process, so they learn to overcome their bias to hide or minimize the risks in their areas of accountability.

Embedded experts
The financial services industry poses a unique challenge because of the volatile dynamics of asset markets and the potential impact of decisions made by decentralized traders and investment

managers. An investment bank's risk profile can change dramatically with a single deal or major market movement. For such companies, risk management requires embedded experts within the organization to continuously monitor and influence the business's risk profile, working side by side with the line managers whose activities are generating new ideas, innovation, and risks—and, if all goes well, profits.

JP Morgan Private Bank adopted this model in 2007, at the onset of the global financial crisis. Risk managers, embedded within the line organization, report to both line executives and a centralized, independent risk-management function. The face-to-face contact with line managers enables the market-savvy risk managers to continually ask "what if" questions, challenging the assumptions of portfolio managers and forcing them to look at different scenarios. Risk managers assess how proposed trades affect the risk of the entire investment portfolio, not only under normal circumstances but also under times of extreme stress, when the correlations of returns across different asset classes escalate. "Portfolio managers come to me with three trades, and the [risk] model may say that all three are adding to the same type of risk," explains Gregoriy Zhikarev, a risk manager at JP Morgan. "Nine times out of 10 a manager will say, 'No, that's not what I want to do.' Then we can sit down and redesign the trades."

The chief danger from embedding risk managers within the line organization is that they "go native," aligning themselves with the inner circle of the business unit's leadership team—becoming deal makers rather than deal questioners. Preventing this is the responsibility of the company's senior risk officer and—ultimately—the CEO, who sets the tone for a company's risk culture.

Avoiding the Function Trap

Even if managers have a system that promotes rich discussions about risk, a second cognitive-behavioral trap awaits them. Because many strategy risks (and some external risks) are quite predictable—even familiar—companies tend to label and compartmentalize them, especially along business function lines. Banks often manage what they label "credit risk," "market risk," and "operational risk" in separate groups. Other companies compartmentalize the management of "brand risk," "reputation risk," "supply chain risk," "human resources risk," "IT risk," and "financial risk."

Such organizational silos disperse both information and responsibility for effective risk management. They inhibit discussion of how different risks interact. Good risk discussions must be not only confrontational but also integrative. Businesses can be derailed by a combination of small events that reinforce one another in unanticipated ways.

Managers can develop a companywide risk perspective by anchoring their discussions in strategic planning, the one integrative process that most well-run companies already have. For example, Infosys, the Indian IT services company, generates risk discussions from the Balanced Scorecard, its management tool for strategy measurement and communication. "As we asked ourselves about what risks we should be looking at," says M. D. Ranganath, the chief risk officer, "we gradually zeroed in on risks to business objectives specified in our corporate scorecard."

In building its Balanced Scorecard, Infosys had identified "growing client relationships" as a key objective and selected metrics for measuring progress, such as the number of global clients with annual billings in excess of $50 million and the annual percentage increases in revenues from large clients. In looking at the goal and the performance metrics together, management realized that its strategy had introduced a new risk factor: client default. When Infosys's business was based on numerous small clients, a single client default would not jeopardize the company's strategy. But a default by a $50 million client would present a major setback. Infosys began to monitor the credit default swap rate of every large client as a leading indicator of the likelihood of default. When a client's rate increased, Infosys would accelerate collection of receivables or request progress payments to reduce the likelihood or impact of default.

To take another example, consider Volkswagen do Brasil (subsequently abbreviated as VW), the Brazilian subsidiary of the

German carmaker. VW's risk-management unit uses the company's strategy map as a starting point for its dialogues about risk. For each objective on the map, the group identifies the risk events that could cause VW to fall short of that objective. The team then generates a Risk Event Card for each risk on the map, listing the practical effects of the event on operations, the probability of occurrence, leading indicators, and potential actions for mitigation. It also identifies who has primary accountability for managing the risk. (See the exhibit "The Risk Event Card.") The risk team then presents a high-level summary of results to senior management. (See the exhibit "The Risk Report Card.")

Beyond introducing a systematic process for identifying and mitigating strategy risks, companies also need a risk oversight structure. Infosys uses a dual structure: a central risk team that identifies general strategy risks and establishes central policy, and specialized functional teams that design and monitor policies and controls in consultation with local business teams. The decentralized teams have the authority and expertise to help the business lines respond to threats and changes in their risk profiles, escalating only the exceptions to the central risk team for review. For example, if a client relationship manager wants to give a longer credit period to a company whose credit risk parameters are high, the functional risk manager can send the case to the central team for review.

These examples show that the size and scope of the risk function are not dictated by the size of the organization. Hydro One, a large company, has a relatively small risk group to generate risk awareness and communication throughout the firm and to advise the executive team on risk-based resource allocations. By contrast, relatively small companies or units, such as JPL or JP Morgan Private Bank, need multiple project-level review boards or teams of embedded risk managers to apply domain expertise to assess the risk of business decisions. And Infosys, a large company with broad operational and strategic scope, requires a strong centralized risk-management function as well as dispersed risk managers who support local business decisions and facilitate the exchange of information with the centralized risk group.

The Risk Event Card

VW do Brasil uses Risk Event Cards to assess its strategy risks. First, managers document the risks associated with achieving each of the company's strategic objectives. For each identified risk, managers create a risk card that lists the practical effects of the event's occurring on operations. Below is a sample card looking at the effects of an interruption in deliveries, which could jeopardize VW's strategic objective of achieving a smoothly functioning supply chain.

Strategic objective	Risk event	Outcomes	Risk indicators	Likelihood/consequences	Management controls	Accountable manager
Guarantee reliable and competitive supplier-to-manufacturer processes	Interruption of deliveries	Overtime Emergency freight Quality problems Production losses	Critical items report Late deliveries Incoming defects Incorrect component shipments		Hold daily supply chain meetings with logistics, purchasing, and QA Monitor suppliers' tooling to detect deterioration Risk mitigation initiative: Upgrade suppliers' tooling Risk mitigation initiative: Identify the key supply chain executive at each critical supplier	Mr. O. Manuel, director of manufacturing logistics

The Risk Report Card

VW do Brasil summarizes its strategy risks on a Risk Report Card organized by strategic objectives (excerpt below). Managers can see at a glance how many of the identified risks for each objective are critical and require attention or mitigation. For instance, VW identified 11 risks associated with achieving the goal "Satisfy the customer's expectations." Four of the risks were critical, but that was an improvement over the previous quarter's assessment. Managers can also monitor progress on risk management across the company.

Strategic objective	Assessed risks	Critical risks	Trend
Achieve market share growth	4	1	⟷
Satisfy the customer's expectations	11	4	⬆
Improve company image	13	1	⟷
Develop dealer organization	4	2	⟷
Guarantee customer-oriented innovations management	5	2	⬇
Achieve launch management efficiency	1	0	⟷
Increase direct processes efficiency	4	1	⟷
Create and manage a robust production volume strategy	2	1	⬇
Guarantee reliable and competitive supplier-to-manufacturer processes	9	3	⟷
Develop an attractive and innovative product portfolio	4	2	⬇

Managing the Uncontrollable

External risks, the third category of risk, cannot typically be reduced or avoided through the approaches used for managing preventable and strategy risks. External risks lie largely outside the company's control; companies should focus on identifying them, assessing their potential impact, and figuring out how best to mitigate their effects should they occur.

65

Some external risk events are sufficiently imminent that managers can manage them as they do their strategy risks. For example, during the economic slowdown after the global financial crisis, Infosys identified a new risk related to its objective of developing a global workforce: an upsurge in protectionism, which could lead to tight restrictions on work visas and permits for foreign nationals in several OECD countries where Infosys had large client engagements. Although protectionist legislation is technically an external risk since it's beyond the company's control, Infosys treated it as a strategy risk and created a Risk Event Card for it, which included a new risk indicator: the number and percentage of its employees with dual citizenships or existing work permits outside India. If this number were to fall owing to staff turnover, Infosys's global strategy might be jeopardized. Infosys therefore put in place recruiting and retention policies that mitigate the consequences of this external risk event.

Most external risk events, however, require a different analytic approach either because their probability of occurrence is very low or because managers find it difficult to envision them during their normal strategy processes. We have identified several different sources of external risks:

- *Natural and economic disasters with immediate impact.* These risks are predictable in a general way, although their timing is usually not (a large earthquake will hit someday in California, but there is no telling exactly where or when). They may be anticipated only by relatively weak signals. Examples include natural disasters such as the 2010 Icelandic volcano eruption that closed European airspace for a week and economic disasters such as the bursting of a major asset price bubble. When these risks occur, their effects are typically drastic and immediate, as we saw in the disruption from the Japanese earthquake and tsunami in 2011.

- *Geopolitical and environmental changes with long-term impact.* These include political shifts such as major policy changes, coups, revolutions, and wars; long-term environmental changes such as global warming; and depletion of critical natural resources such as fresh water.

- *Competitive risks with medium-term impact.* These include the emergence of disruptive technologies (such as the internet, smartphones, and bar codes) and radical strategic moves by industry players (such as the entry of Amazon into book retailing and Apple into the mobile phone and consumer electronics industries).

Companies use different analytic approaches for each of the sources of external risk.

Tail-risk stress tests

Stress-testing helps companies assess major changes in one or two specific variables whose effects would be major and immediate, although the exact timing is not forecastable. Financial services firms use stress tests to assess, for example, how an event such as the tripling of oil prices, a large swing in exchange or interest rates, or the default of a major institution or sovereign country would affect trading positions and investments.

The benefits from stress-testing, however, depend critically on the assumptions—which may themselves be biased—about how much the variable in question will change. The tail-risk stress tests of many banks in 2007-2008, for example, assumed a worst-case scenario in which U.S. housing prices leveled off and remained flat for several periods. Very few companies thought to test what would happen if prices began to decline—an excellent example of the tendency to anchor estimates in recent and readily available data. Most companies extrapolated from recent U.S. housing prices, which had gone several decades without a general decline, to develop overly optimistic market assessments.

Scenario planning

This tool is suited for long-range analysis, typically five to 10 years out. Originally developed at Shell Oil in the 1960s, scenario analysis is a systematic process for defining the plausible boundaries of future states of the world. Participants examine political, economic, technological, social, regulatory, and environmental forces and select some number of drivers—typically four—that would have the biggest impact on the company. Some companies explicitly draw on the expertise in their advisory boards to inform them about significant trends, outside the company's and industry's day-to-day focus, that should be considered in their scenarios.

For each of the selected drivers, participants estimate maximum and minimum anticipated values over five to 10 years. Combining the extreme values for each of four drivers leads to 16 scenarios. About half tend to be implausible and are discarded; participants then assess how their firm's strategy would perform in the remaining scenarios. If managers see that their strategy is contingent on a generally optimistic view, they can modify it to accommodate pessimistic scenarios or develop plans for how they would change their strategy should early indicators show an increasing likelihood of events turning against it.

War-gaming

War-gaming assesses a firm's vulnerability to disruptive technologies or changes in competitors' strategies. In a war-game, the company assigns three or four teams the task of devising plausible near-term strategies or actions that existing or potential competitors might adopt during the next one or two years—a shorter time horizon than that of scenario analysis. The teams then meet to examine how clever competitors could attack the company's strategy. The process helps to overcome the bias of leaders to ignore evidence that runs counter to their current beliefs, including the possibility of actions that competitors might take to disrupt their strategy.

Companies have no influence over the likelihood of risk events identified through methods such as tail-risk testing, scenario planning, and war-gaming. But managers can take specific actions to mitigate their impact. Since moral hazard does not arise for non-preventable events, companies can use insurance or hedging to mitigate some risks, as an airline does when it protects itself against sharp increases in fuel prices by using financial derivatives. Another option is for firms to make investments now to avoid much higher costs later. For instance, a manufacturer with facilities in earthquake-prone areas can increase its construction costs to protect critical facilities against severe quakes. Also, companies exposed to different but comparable risks can cooperate to mitigate them. For example, the IT data centers of a university in North Carolina would be vulnerable to hurricane risk while those of a comparable university on the San Andreas Fault in California would be vulnerable to earthquakes. The likelihood that both disasters would happen on the same day is small enough that the two universities might choose to mitigate their risks by backing up each other's systems every night.

The Leadership Challenge

Managing risk is very different from managing strategy. Risk management focuses on the negative—threats and failures rather than opportunities and successes. It runs exactly counter to the "can do" culture most leadership teams try to foster when implementing strategy. And many leaders have a tendency to discount the future; they're reluctant to spend time and money now to avoid an uncertain future problem that might occur down the road, on someone else's watch. Moreover, mitigating risk typically involves dispersing resources and diversifying investments, just the opposite of the intense focus of a successful strategy. Managers may find it antithetical to their culture to champion processes that identify the risks to the strategies they helped formulate.

For those reasons, most companies need a separate function to handle strategy- and external-risk management. The risk function's size will vary from company to company, but the group must report directly to the top team. Indeed, nurturing a close relationship with senior leadership will arguably be its most critical task; a company's ability to weather storms depends very much on how seriously executives take their risk-management function when the sun is shining and no clouds are on the horizon.

That was what separated the banks that failed in the financial crisis from those that survived. The failed companies had relegated risk management to a compliance function; their risk managers had limited access to senior management and their boards of directors. Further, executives routinely ignored risk managers' warnings about highly leveraged and concentrated positions. By contrast, Goldman Sachs and JPMorgan Chase, two firms that weathered the financial crisis well, had strong internal risk-management functions and leadership teams that understood and managed the companies' multiple risk exposures. Barry Zubrow, chief risk officer at JP Morgan Chase, told us, "I may have the title, but [CEO] Jamie Dimon is the chief risk officer of the company."

Risk management is nonintuitive; it runs counter to many individual and organizational biases. Rules and compliance can mitigate some critical risks but not all of them. Active and cost-effective risk management requires managers to think systematically about the multiple categories of risks they face so that they can institute appropriate processes for each. These processes will neutralize their managerial bias of seeing the world as they would like it to be rather than as it actually is or could possibly become.

Originally published in June 2012. Reprint R1206B

Surviving Disruption

by Maxwell Wessel and Clayton M. Christensen

DISRUPTIVE INNOVATIONS ARE LIKE MISSILES launched at your business. For 20 years we've described missile after missile that took aim and annihilated its target: Napster, Amazon, and the Apple Store devastated Tower Records and Musicland; tiny, underpowered personal computers grew to replace minicomputers and mainframes; digital photography made film practically obsolete.

And all along we've prescribed a single response to ensure that when the dust settles, you'll still have a viable business: Develop a disruption of your own before it's too late to reap the rewards of participation in new, high-growth markets—as Procter & Gamble did with Swiffer, Dow Corning with Xiameter, and Apple with the iPod, iTunes, the iPad, and (most spectacularly) the iPhone. That prescription is, if anything, even more imperative in an increasingly volatile world.

But it is also incomplete.

Disruption is less a single event than a process that plays out over time, sometimes quickly and completely, but other times slowly and incompletely. More than a century after the invention of air transport, cargo ships still crisscross the globe. More than 40 years after Southwest Airlines went public, tens of thousands of passengers fly daily with legacy carriers. A generation after the introduction of the VCR, box-office receipts are still an enormous component of film revenues. Managers must not only disrupt themselves but also consider the fate of their legacy operations, for which decades or more of profitability may lie ahead.

We propose a systematic way to chart the path and pace of disruption so that you can fashion a more complete strategic response. To determine whether a missile will hit you dead-on, graze you, or pass you altogether, you need to:

- Identify the strengths of your disrupter's business model

- Identify your own relative advantages

- Evaluate the conditions that would help or hinder the disrupter from co-opting your current advantages in the future

To guide you in determining a disrupter's strengths, we introduce the concept of the *extendable core*—the aspect of its business model that allows the disrupter to maintain its performance advantage as it creeps upmarket in search of more and more customers. We then explore how a deep understanding of what jobs people want your company to do for them—and what jobs the disrupter could do better

---

LEGACY BUSINESS   **DISRUPTER**

Handheld GPS Cell Phone GPS

**WHAT JOBS DO CUSTOMERS
WANT THIS PRODUCT TO PERFORM?**

"Inform me about my surroundings"   "Get me to the meeting on time"   "Get me home safely"

In case of emergency, people still value the reliability of a rugged, waterproof GPS device with a long battery life, so creating durable devices with even longer-lasting batteries may help secure this niche. But disrupters may overcome new-technology barriers to making those improvements.

EASY TO DISRUPT

DISRUPTER ADVANTAGES

GPS apps are included in the smartphone price

GPS data are easily integrated with information from other apps, such as restaurant reviews and reservation systems

DISRUPTER DISADVANTAGES

Phones are fragile

Phones must be small enough to fit into a pocket, restricting their size and weight

Batteries must be recharged more frequently because the phones are used for other tasks

---

Idea in Brief

Not all disruptive missiles are destined to hit you directly or right away. Disruptions that will not greatly affect you for years require you to consider the right path forward for your core business.

To do so, you need to identify (1) the disrupter's advantage, (2) your own advantage, and (3) how easily the disrupter might co-opt your advantage in the future.

New insights into the mechanism of disruption reveal that the disrupter's advantage stems from its *extendable core*—its ability to maintain radically lower prices as it creeps upmarket in search of more customers. Your advantage stems from how well you do the jobs your customers want you to do. Your prospects for the future depend on adjusting your current business model to perform those jobs better and on how likely the disrupter is to overcome the fundamental barriers in its path.

with its extendable core—will give you a clearer picture of your relative advantage. We go on to delineate the barriers a disrupter would need to overcome to undermine you in the future. This approach will enable you to see which parts of your current business are most vulnerable to disruption and—just as important—which parts you can defend.

Where Advantage Lies

What makes an innovation disruptive? As our colleague Michael Raynor suggested in his book *The Innovator's Manifesto* (2011), all disruptive innovations stem from technological or business model advantages that can scale as disruptive businesses move upmarket in search of more-demanding customers. These advantages are what enable the extendable core; they differentiate disruption from mere price competition.

To understand this important distinction, consider Raynor's example of simple price competition in the hotel industry: A Holiday Inn provides a bed for the night for less (and in less luxury) than does the Four Seasons down the street. For the economy hotel chain to appeal to Four Seasons customers, it would have to invest in internal improvements, prime real estate, and an expensive service staff.

Doing so would force it to adopt the same cost structure as the Four Seasons, so it would have to charge its customers similarly.

By contrast, in a disruptive innovation, an upstart can maintain its advantage while it improves its performance. What made the PC a disruptive innovation rather than just a low-end minicomputer, for instance, was the radical cost advantage its manufacturers achieved when they assembled their machines using standardized components. As component makers steadily improved the price and performance of their offerings, PC makers could preserve (or increase) their cost advantage even as they increased the power, capacity, and utility of their machines. This option was unavailable to minicomputer makers, because their improvements were derived from ever more effective designs of costly custom systems.

Not all the advantages of a disrupter's extendable core are so overpowering; often they are offset by disadvantages. Take the current disruption of higher education. Online universities can enroll, educate, and grant degrees to far more students at much lower cost than traditional institutions of higher learning can, because e-learning technologies enable every faculty member to reach far more people than any single professor could address in even the largest university lecture hall. The initial quality of e-learning institutions left something to be desired, but—as the theory of disruption predicts—they have been improving the effectiveness of their programs while maintaining their cost and convenience advantages, thus attracting more students away from traditional alternatives.

But consider two groups of students these online universities have difficulty serving. One group is those who are looking to burnish their résumés by demonstrating that they are good enough to get into an exclusive college. The online universities' extendable core is not much use here because their advantage lies in serving ever greater numbers of students with the same material—hardly a demonstration of exclusivity.

The other group is students who value the social aspects of college: the growth opportunities in living away from home, the close community of peers, the storied sports teams. E-learning institutions can (and do) opt to offer both online and on-campus courses in order to attract the widest variety of students, but they can't bring their full disruptive advantage to bear here, because each added service forces them further toward the cost structure of traditional universities. Novel partnerships or technological innovations might eventually enable them to address this problem, but their extendable core in its current form falls short of satisfying these students.

Identifying a disrupter's extendable core tells you what kinds of customers the disrupter might attract and—just as important—what kinds it won't. How many customers of each kind do you have? To answer that question, you need to consider what people are really doing when they buy your products and services.

Where Advantage Matters

Why do people long for certain products and services in some situations but not in others? Experts in disruption have a ready answer: to complete some job that crops up in their lives. A college student doesn't go shopping for floor cleaner, sponges, and a bucket for their own sake. Something—say, the impending arrival of his parents—makes it necessary for him to clean his room, so he seeks some product or service with which to do it. The floor cleaner, sponges, and bucket have no intrinsic value for him. It's their ability to keep him on good terms with his family that he cares about.

Successful entrepreneurs naturally look at opportunities in terms of the jobs they can do for customers. An innovator observing the plight of our student might realize that he doesn't care about keeping his room clean all the time, so he's not interested in stocking up on cleaning supplies. Because he doesn't clean often and may not be good at it, he's probably looking for something simple and foolproof. And he has probably waited to clean until just before his parents arrive (so that his room will stay neat), which means he needs to do the job quickly. An enterprising fellow student might see that as an opportunity to start a 30-minute emergency cleaning service on campus. A consumer goods company might consider bundling small amounts of appropriate cleaning supplies and making them conveniently available at university bookstores, nearby pharmacies, or even coffee shops.

Identifying what jobs people need done and how they could be done more easily, conveniently, or affordably is what enables a disrupter to imagine how to improve its product to appeal to more and more of your customers. If you can determine how effective or ineffective the disrupter is likely to be at doing the jobs you currently do, you can identify the most vulnerable segments of your core business—and your most sustainable advantages. When a disruptive business offers a significant advantage and no disadvantages in doing the same job you do, disruption will be swift and complete (think online music versus CDs). But when the advantages of a disrupter's extendable core are ill suited to doing that job and its disadvantages are considerable, disruption will be slower and incomplete. Thus, at the simplest level, cargo ships are still in use because they're still much better than planes at transporting heavy goods. Box-office receipts still represent a large portion of studio revenues in part because sizable groups of people (teenage boys, dating couples) go to the movies to get out of the house. Ivy League universities are still better positioned than online institutions to confer elite status on aspiring high school seniors.

When Advantage Persists

Could something happen to make cargo ships obsolete or to decrease the value of an elite education? To find out, we need to consider how easily a disrupter could overcome its disadvantages in the future— to ask, "What would have to change for my current advantages to evaporate?" To approach this question, we propose a systematic assessment of five kinds of barriers to disruption, arranged here from easiest to overcome to hardest.

1. The momentum barrier (customers are used to the status quo)

2. The tech-implementation barrier (which could be overcome using existing technology)

3. The ecosystem barrier (which would require a change in the business environment to overcome)

4. The new-technologies barrier (the technology needed to change the competitive landscape does not yet exist)

5. The business model barrier (the disrupter would have to adopt your cost structure)

The more difficult the barrier, or the more barriers a disrupter faces, the more likely it is that customers will remain with incumbents. Cargo ships, whose containers are designed to move seamlessly from quay to rail to truck to loading dock, benefit from an ecosystem barrier, which airlines might conceivably assault with an integrated system of their own. Far more formidable, of course, is the new-technologies barrier to developing cheap, renewable jet fuel, which would enable airlines to dramatically lower the cost of air shipping.

LEGACY BUSINESS
Auto Sales

DISRUPTER
Car Sharing

WHAT JOBS DO CUSTOMERS WANT THIS PRODUCT TO PERFORM?

"Get my kids safely to school"	"Help me get where I need to go when I need to go there"	"Provide a mobile office"

Drivers who work in their cars value the ability to store and optimally arrange papers, laptops, luggage, and other items. Moving them from car to car would be highly inconvenient and time-consuming, so car sharing is unlikely to overcome this business model barrier any time soon.

HARD TO DISRUPT

DISRUPTER ADVANTAGES

More cost-effective than ownership for infrequent drivers

No need for insurance

Parking is included

Users can drive a variety of makes and models

DISRUPTER DISADVANTAGES

Less cost-effective than ownership for frequent and long-distance drivers

Cars aren't always available when needed

This approach may seem intuitive, but decades of training have taught executives to focus not on the value they provide for their customers but on proxies for it—high-level profit and revenue data. If an innovator is causing a company losses, it's deemed threatening. If not, it's often dismissed. And overestimating a threat can be as costly as ignoring it: Managers struggle to keep customers who are unlikely to be lost to disruption in the same way they would compete with traditional rivals—by dropping prices or offering comparable product features. This sort of response both fails to identify the intrinsic advantage of the disrupter and ignores advantages that the legacy business could viably defend.

To many, it may be clear why ships still carry cargo and why the disruption of the movie theater by DVDs is incomplete. However, that clarity is easier to achieve in retrospect than it was on the precipice of disruption. During the 1980s content producers were up in arms over the spread of home video distribution. Today those same studios are fighting frantically to limit the adoption of digital streaming—which, although it certainly represents an improvement over (and a direct threat to) DVDs, remains at a distinct disadvantage in doing many of the jobs that movie theaters still perform.

To demonstrate how our approach can be applied both in more-ambiguous cases and in a prescriptive fashion, let's turn to a disruption that's occurring right now.

The Disruption of Retail Grocery Stores

Over the past 15 years online retailing has devastated traditional brick-and-mortar retailers. The disruption began with the swift destruction of companies such as Tower Records and Hollywood Video and has taken its toll on high-margin retailers like Neiman Marcus and Saks Fifth Avenue. Retail continues to be a hotbed of entrepreneurship and innovation.

One of the last bastions against this disruptive wave is the grocery industry. Only about 1% of all groceries in the United States are bought from online retailers like Peapod, NetGrocer, and Fresh-Direct. However, we can expect that with an incentive to innovate their way upmarket, e-grocers will become increasingly significant. The theory of disruption tells us that these entrants will speed their delivery times, increase their product selection, and add features we can hardly imagine today in pursuit of new customers and higher profit margins. Even now, Amazon is making more and more grocery staples available online and is experimenting with discounted prices for automatic replenishment services. And Walmart has constructed convenient urban pickup centers for items bought online.

Questions for the executives of Kroger, Safeway, Whole Foods, and the like are "How complete will the grocery industry's disruption become?" and "What role will traditional brick-and-mortar stores play in the grocery market of the future?"

Online Grocers' Extendable Core

We all intuitively grasp the advantages of online retailing. But for businesses attempting to predict the extent and impact of disruption, intuition isn't always enough. When Amazon first opened its virtual doors, most people saw only its most salient advantage—the deep price discounts it could offer by passing along the cost savings it gained from dispensing with physical retail outlets. A more careful analysis of its business model revealed that cash flow was an even greater advantage: Consumers gave Amazon their money before Amazon had to pay its suppliers for inventory. (This was so lucrative that it helped to fund much of Amazon's early development.) Conceivably, anything sold online, whether books or cornflakes, has a similar advantage. Online grocers can reduce their inventory by centralizing warehouses and can pay less for products than traditional grocery chains do by purchasing them on an even greater scale. They don't have to pay costly sales staff. And sometimes, through careful warehouse placement, they can avoid paying state sales taxes.

On the downside, though, online grocers have to ship their products to individual homes—far more destinations than any brick-and-mortar grocer need worry about. They must manage complex logistics chains to coordinate shipments of the various items that make up a grocery order, whereas supermarket shoppers merely toss everything into a cart and wheel it to the front of the store. The lack of sales staff limits customer service for online grocers. And for consumers, the convenience of shopping from home comes at the expense of direct physical contact with the goods.

Which of these advantages and disadvantages do the managers at Kroger and Whole Foods need to focus on? To answer that question, they must discover just how shoppers are using their stores.

The Jobs Brick-and-Mortar Grocers Do

We find that the best way to identify the jobs a company does for its customers is through a combination of extensive surveys, interviews, focus groups, and in-person observations. Spend a day near

LEGACY BUSINESS **Railroads**	DISRUPTER **Cars, Trucks, and Planes**	DISRUPTER ADVANTAGES
WHAT JOBS DO CUSTOMERS WANT THIS SERVICE TO PERFORM?		Roads connect far more places than rail lines do
"Help me get home for the holidays" / "Get my products to customers quickly" / "Help me operate my business efficiently"		Trucks can more easily deliver items from any factory to any destination on a road
		Airplanes can move people and cargo much faster than rail can
Manufacturers value rail's far lower cost so much that they locate factories on a rail line. For many customers this business model advantage currently outweighs both the speed advantage of airplanes and the flexibility advantage of trucks. So standardized rail containers, which can be stacked and easily transferred to ships or trucks, create a powerful ecosystem barrier to disruption. **HARD TO DISRUPT**		Airplanes can move people and cargo overseas
		DISRUPTER DISADVANTAGES Higher variable costs Higher labor costs

a Kroger exit, and you'll see a few distinct patterns. In the morning and early afternoon, many customers spend a substantial amount of time in all the store's aisles loading up large grocery carts. Occasionally a customer zips in to buy one or two items and checks out in the express lane. Late in the afternoon, a handful of customers are still filling their carts with staples, but far more are picking up fresh vegetables, proteins, and the occasional baked good.

At the end of the day, if you had taken notes and interviewed a few customers about what they came to the store to accomplish (and what alternatives they use for the same purpose), you'd probably be ready to identify at least some of the jobs customers were hiring Kroger to complete. The people filling their carts were stocking up on products they knew in advance they would need—the weekly grocery pickup. The ones zipping in and out were after some emergency item they'd forgotten or something essential sold only by that market. The shoppers arriving during the afternoon rush were gathering ingredients for that night's dinner. These three jobs are by no means comprehensive, but they are big enough drivers of the customer population to shed light on the pace of grocery's disruption and on what the industry will look like in its wake.

You might assume that this sort of intention analysis is common, but it happens far less often than it should. Advances in data collection and analysis have made it possible to get ever more detailed information about who's buying, what they're buying, how often they're buying, and whom they're with when they're buying. Typically, consulting firms and internal strategy teams take reams of such data, crunch the numbers, and organize people into segments such as "frequent shoppers," "young parents," and "discount hunters." These labels appear to be aimed at uncovering intentions, but they essentially remain descriptions of types of people, and thus tell us little about behavior in certain circumstances.

For instance, at the onset of a disruption, we might know that Kroger's most frequent shoppers were young mothers, but we wouldn't know what they were doing when they came into the store. The same woman might on one occasion walk methodically up and down the aisles, stocking up on the week's nonperishables, and on another might be dashing in to grab a forgotten item or two. She might also be returning practically every evening at 5:30 to buy the ingredients for that night's dinner. Or not. Without an understanding of what she's trying to accomplish each time she visits, it's impossible to identify what innovations might matter to her when she walks through the door.

Once you understand what jobs customers most commonly hire you to do, it becomes much easier to begin evaluating how important the advantages and disadvantages of a disrupter's extendable core are to your business. Take the job of providing emergency goods. Imagine that it's 8:45 p.m. and you've just realized that you're out of toothpaste. You immediately head to a store to ensure that you'll avoid the costly impact of gingivitis. You're not thinking about the advantages of shopping from home, the selection offered by nearly infinite shelf space, or the low price afforded by scale. You're focused on instant delivery. In deciding which store to visit, you find yourself comparing the traditional competitive advantages of physical retailers such as 7-Eleven, CVS, and the supermarket. The decision comes down to which of those stores is closest to you and whether you think it will have your favorite toothpaste (or at least an acceptable alternative) in stock. In this situation an online retailer's advantages are simply not relevant to you.

Consider the job of buying dinner, and you'll reach a similar conclusion about the relative advantages of brick-and-mortar markets over online retailing. Interviews with shoppers who are picking up dinner ingredients reveal that they typically don't decide what they're going to buy until they're at the store. Many use the store's selection to narrow down the possibilities—seeing what looks appealing helps them with the task of planning dinner day after day. They are likely to place a high value on obtaining the freshest ingredients. Because each tomato, steak, or bunch of grapes is different, they want to pick up and examine the perishable ingredients they're considering. Although FreshDirect and Peapod may guarantee freshness, these shoppers feel comforted by seeing the product in person. Only a compelling offer, such as Gilt Taste's gourmet products at steeply reduced prices, can substitute for their own judgment. Absent such a strong point of differentiation, customers turn to supermarkets, farmers' markets, and corner stores to get the job done. The convenience of online retail is simply not enough.

Just as we can envision the difficulties a disrupter would have in completing the emergency-item and dinner-shopping jobs, we can see how vulnerable the staples-shopping job is. Shoppers stocking up on branded nonperishables such as canned tuna, coffee, pancake mix, and spaghetti sauce know what they want and generally don't require it immediately. A sizable number of them already wait until they need a sufficient quantity to justify a trip to BJ's or Costco. Shopping on Amazon and waiting a few days for the items to be delivered is not so different. This is the job, our analysis suggests, that is most susceptible to disruption by online grocers. The early successes of Diapers.com and Soap.com in selling branded nonperishables traditionally provided by physical grocery stores is a harbinger of the coming shift.

The Barriers to Disruption

We can see disruption on the horizon, but how close is it? Returning to the five barriers—momentum, tech implementation, ecosystem, new technologies, business model—we can see that for online grocers to overcome their disadvantage in doing the job of providing emergency goods, they would have to engage in a costly infrastructure extension, either to build their own stores and adopt their traditional competitors' cost structures, or to send delivery trucks out at nowhere near optimum capacity. So for this job, disrupters are hitting the formidable business model barrier. Because either change would destroy their advantage, we can label this disadvantage significant and difficult to overcome.

A disrupter that is trying to do the job of stocking up on staples clearly encounters no business model barrier, no new-technology barrier, no genuine tech-implementation barrier, and a weakening momentum barrier. Still, one could argue that daily trips to the grocery store for dinner or emergency items might make the thought of shopping online for nonperishables seem duplicative. But this is true only as long as it makes sense to shop at traditional grocery stores.

What if farmers' markets continue to proliferate, or if a traditional competitor—say, Trader Joe's—chooses to invest in smaller-format urban grocery stores that feature fewer staples and more fresh goods? Then it may well become sensible for consumers to shop for nonperishables separately. Because we can envision that such an ecosystem shift will result naturally from entrepreneurs' pursuit of profit, we predict that disruption will arrive sooner rather than later.

The Path Forward

Online grocers constitute a viable and potent threat when it comes to the job of delivering products we know in advance that we need. Customers who hire traditional grocers to do that job already value the broad selection and lower prices that online grocers are poised to provide. Over time, as they get used to shopping online, they may also come to value free delivery and the savings on gasoline they achieve by eliminating errands. As more customers adopt the online format, it will become ever more difficult for brick-and-mortar grocers to compete here. Legacy grocers could establish discount programs, secure exclusive distribution, put bigger stores in more-convenient locations, institute or expand loyalty programs that offer savings on gas to retain shoppers who are looking to stock up. But ultimately those efforts will be futile. As online grocers grow in scale, they will be able to offer better discount programs, match loyalty programs, work to secure the same exclusive distribution. Wise brick-and-mortar grocers won't fight this disruption head-on. They will instead focus on developing innovations aimed at completing their still-defensible jobs—serving the emergency shopper and the harried soul who is trying to put dinner on the table.

To better serve those customers, traditional grocery retailers should focus on outcompeting convenience stores with lower prices and better quality (particularly of perishables) and outcompeting farmers' markets—perhaps with greater selection or by enticing farmers to sell produce inside their stores. They should be thinking hard about their physical advantages—considering how store layouts might help or hinder the shopper who is trying to gather ingredients for dinner. They might mimic England's Marks & Spencer by offering high-end semiprepared meals to recapture some of the margin lost from shrinking sales of branded nonperishables. Some might even experiment with locating shelf space inside other conveniently located retail outlets: A branded Trader Joe's aisle inside CVS would allow both retailers to better serve customers. Knowing where you're likely to succeed and where you're not is the key to making critical resource allocation decisions—not in the service of ephemeral short-term margins but in the realistic pursuit of longer-term competitive advantage.

The missiles of disruption are aimed at your local Kroger, Whole Foods, and Safeway. Their leaders should expect increasing competition from online upstarts for the highly profitable branded items that currently fill so many supermarket aisles. They would do well to plan for a world in which those revenues are in some large part lost to them forever.

Accepting the existence of a new competitive paradigm is never easy. It often forces us to acknowledge an inevitable loss of business. It may require us to develop disruptions that cannibalize our existing businesses. Failing to come to terms with these realities does us no service.

But neither does prematurely convincing ourselves of the singular superiority of a competitor's disruptive advantages. After all, Kroger, Whole Foods, and Safeway still perform important functions for millions of people that no online grocer will be able to perform anytime soon. Before leaders engage in reckless price competition or squander resources and effort in the futile defense of lost causes, they owe it to their shareholders, employees, and customers to take stock of the entire situation and respond comprehensively—to meet disrupters with disruption of their own, but also to guide their legacy businesses toward as healthy a future as possible.

Originally published in December 2012. Reprint R1212C

The Great Repeatable Business Model

by Chris Zook and James Allen

DIFFERENTIATION IS THE essence of strategy, the prime source of competitive advantage. You earn money not just by performing a valuable task but by being different from your competitors in a manner that lets you serve your core customers better and more profitably.

The sharper your differentiation, the greater your advantage. Consider Tetra Pak, a company that in 2010 sold more than 150 billion packages in 170 markets around the world. Tetra Pak's carton packages extend the shelf life of products and eliminate the need for refrigeration. The shapes they take—squares and pyramids, for example—stack more efficiently in trucks and on shelves than most cans or bottles. The packaging machines that use the company's unique laminated material lend themselves to high-volume dairy operations. These three features set Tetra Pak well apart from its competitors and allow it to produce a package that more than compensates for its cost.

In studying companies that sustained a high level of performance over many years, we found that more than 80% of them had this kind of well-defined and easily understood differentiation at the center of their strategy. Nike's differentiation resides in the power of its brand, the company's relationships with top athletes, and its signature performance-focused product design. Singapore Air's differentiation comes from its unique ways of providing premium service at a reasonable cost on long-haul business flights. Apple's differentiation consists of deep capabilities in writing easy-to-use software, the integrated iTunes system, and a simplicity of design and product line (Apple has only about 60 main SKUs).

You can find high performers like these in most industries. The cold truth about hot markets is this: Over the long run, a company's strategic differentiation and execution matter far more to its performance—our research suggests at least four times as much—than the business it happens to be in. Every industry has leaders and laggards, and the leaders are typically the most highly differentiated.

But differentiation tends to wear with age, and not just because competitors try hard to undermine or replicate it. Often the real problem is internal: The growth generated by successful differentiation begets complexity, and a complex company tends to forget what it's good at. Products proliferate. Acquisitions take it far from its core. Frontline employees, more and more distant from the CEO's office, lose their sense of the company's strategic priorities. A lack of consistency kills economies of scale and retards the company's ability to learn. Small wonder that "reinvention" and "disruption" have become leading buzzwords; companies struggling with complexity and fading differentiation come to believe they must reimagine their entire business models quickly and dramatically or else be overwhelmed by upstarts with disruptive innovations.

Most of the time, however, reinvention is the wrong way to go. Our experience, supported by more than 15 years of research into high performance, has led us to the inescapable conclusion that most really successful companies do not reinvent themselves through periodic "binge and purge" strategies. Instead they relentlessly build on their fundamental differentiation, going from strength to strength. They learn to deliver their differentiation to the front line, creating an organization that lives and breathes its strategic advantages day in and day out. They learn how to sustain it over time through constant adaptation to changes in the market. And they learn to resist the siren song of the *idée du jour* better than their less focused competitors. The result is a simple, repeatable business model that a company can apply to new products and markets over

Idea in Brief

Really successful companies build their strategies on a few vivid and hardy forms of differentiation that act as a system and reinforce one another.

They grow in ways that exploit their core differentiators by replicating them in new contexts. And they turn the sources of their differentiation into routines, behaviors, and activity systems that everyone in the organization can understand and follow.

Powerful differentiations deliver enduring profits only when they are supported by simple, non-negotiable principles and robust learning systems that drive constant improvement across the business.

and over again to generate sustained growth. The simplicity means that everyone in the company is on the same page—and no one forgets the sources of success.

Let's look in more detail at what this involves.

Sources of Differentiation

Opportunities for differentiation are rich and varied in virtually every industry. To examine them more closely, we built a database of 8,000 global companies and tracked their performance over 25 years. We created another database of 200 global companies, which we studied in detail. We supplemented that research with two other data sets: a survey conducted with the Economist Intelligence Unit of nearly 400 global executives, and 50 interviews with chief executives around the world. Building on the data, we cataloged 250 assets or capabilities that can contribute to differentiation and sorted them into three major clusters of five categories each. (See the sidebar "The Differentiation Map.")

The most enduring performers, we found, built their strategy on a few vivid, robust forms of differentiation that acted as a system, reinforcing one another. To illustrate, let's examine the factors that make the mutual fund company Vanguard one of the most consistently high-performing businesses in our study.

Ever since its founding, in 1974, Vanguard has been a different kind of company. Its founder, John Bogle, believed passionately in the value of index funds. He saw that a company based on them would need few fund managers and researchers and could therefore charge considerably less than companies with actively managed funds. Bogle also felt he should deal directly with customers and offer them highly responsive service, thus building loyalty. These characteristics are at the core of Vanguard's differentiation today, as can be seen in "The Differentiation Map." The company has the lowest-cost mutual fund "engine," a distribution system that avoids middlemen and allows direct contact with customers, and the highest level of customer loyalty in the industry.

The strongest sources of differentiation in a company's strongest businesses are its crown jewels. Yet our research shows that most management teams spend little time discussing or measuring them and therefore don't agree on what they are. This lack of clarity permeates entire organizations. For instance, more than half of frontline employees say in surveys that they are not clear on their companies' strategic tenets and differentiators. Customers are even more mystified: Although 80% of managers told us they thought their companies were strongly differentiated, fewer than 10% of customers agreed. Yet understanding and agreeing about differentiation, where it can be applied, and how it must evolve is what makes a strategy work.

The Differentiation Map

WE CATALOGED 250 ASSETS or capabilities that can make up a company's differentiation. We then sorted them into three major clusters, each with five categories, to create the Differentiation Map. Assuming that four or five categories are required to achieve differentiation, these 15 basic categories generate more than 5,000 distinct ways in which a company can differentiate itself. (It is possible, however, to break the categories down further, in which case the number of ways to differentiate explodes into more than a million.)

Vanguard's differentiating strengths are highlighted on the next page.

	Management systems	Operating capabilities	Proprietary assets
Back-office ↑	Portfolio management and finance	Supply chain and logistics	Tangible assets
	M&A, joint ventures, and partnering Unique setup as a "mutual company of mutual funds"	**Production and operations** Lowest-cost, no-load mutual fund "engine" skewed to index funds	Scale
	Regulatory management	Development and innovation	Technology and IP
	Business unit strategy and driving priorities	**Go-to-market** Direct distribution, avoiding middleman when possible	Brand
Customer-facing ↓	HR management and culture	**Customer relationships** Loyalty leader for strong customer service; no outsourcing	Tied customer network

A systematic approach to understanding your sources of differentiation is key to rectifying this situation. It enables you to have a meaningful discussion of what distinguishes your company from competitors and what you can build on. When we ask each of a company's top 15 managers privately what he or she feels are the most differentiated and important assets and capabilities, we often find a surprising lack of agreement.

One way to bring data to bear on this range of views is to rate the success of your company's past 20 growth investments and determine what they have in common. This is a starting point for mapping the company's differentiation. Discussions of what really differentiates a business from its competitors are, however, often based on past beliefs more than on current data. As you deliberate about your own key differentiators, you might consult these criteria: Are they (1) truly distinctive? (2) measurable against competitors? (3) relevant to what you deliver to your core customers? (4) mutually reinforcing? (5) clear at all levels of the company? Though each of the five seems obvious, reaching agreement on your differentiation and testing it against these criteria is not as easy as it sounds. The harder it proves, the more valuable the exercise. In our experience, many companies fail these tests—but the most successful ones pass them every time.

The ability to recognize and test the sources of your differentiation in this way is important for focusing innovation. Most innovations, even disruptive ones, affect only one part of a business model, leaving the rest intact. The shift from glasses to contact lenses, for example, had little effect on the basic customer need for vision correction, the industry's distribution system, or the network of eye doctors. The shift from wired to wireless telephony caused chaos for many incumbents, yet some used their infrastructure, customer access, brand, and ability to work with regulatory organizations to prevail. The more precise your understanding of your model and the sources of its success, the more precisely you can focus innovation resources on the areas where the threats and the need for change are greatest.

Making Your Differentiation Easier to Repeat

REPLICATING YOUR GREATEST SUCCESSES means deeply understanding their root causes, maintaining a 360-degree view of where they could be adapted, and ensuring that the entire organization internalizes the strategy and the differentiation on which they are built. Here are six actions to consider:

1. **Make sure that you and your management team agree** on your differentiation now and in the future. You may want to ask each person to write it down; then you can collate the results in advance for discussion. At a minimum, consider three questions: (a) What do our core customers see as our key sources of competitive differentiation? (b) How do we know? (c) Are these sources becoming more or less robust?

2. **See whether the front line of your organization agrees** with what you come up with. Can employees and supervisors describe the strategy and the areas of differentiation as you do? Do they feel that they understand the strategy? Is it simple and clear? Online surveys, anonymously tabulated, can be a big help with this task.

3. **Write your strategy on a page,** or even on an index card. Does your description of it center on the key sources of differentiation? Is your page sharp and convincing to others, including customers and investors, and backed by data?

4. **Conduct a postmortem** of your 20 most recent growth investments and initiatives. Are your greatest successes or disappointments explained, in part, by the central differentiators that were transferred?

5. **Translate your strategy** into a few nonnegotiables. Can you describe simple principles that the organization believes in and that define the key behaviors, beliefs, and values needed to drive the strategy? Are they embedded in day-to-day routines, or are they simply words on a page?

6. **Review how you monitor** the most important health indicators of your core business and its differentiators, both for short-term adjustment and for long-term investment in new capabilities. Does your method drive learning and adaptation? Is quickness to adapt a competitive advantage? Are you sure?

Growth Based in Differentiation

The best way to grow is usually by replicating your strongest strategic advantage in new contexts. Companies typically expand in one or more of four ways: They create or purchase new products and services, create or enter new customer segments, enter new geographic locations, or enter related lines of business. A company can pursue each of these strategies in various ways—for example, adding new price points or finding new uses for a product or service that will appeal to new customers.

The power of a repeatable model lies in the way it turns the sources of differentiation into routines, behaviors, and activity systems that everyone in the organization can understand and follow so that when a company sets out on a particular growth path, it knows how to maintain the differentiation that led to its initial success. The global agribusiness Olam is a case in point. The company began as a cashew trader. It purchased nuts directly from farmers in Nigeria and sold them to a dozen customers in Europe, managing a supply chain from the farm gate to the shop door. This approach was unusual for the industry. It cut out middlemen, safeguarded Olam's access to products, and increased the company's market intelligence and speed of reaction. To do this well, of course, Olam had to learn to work closely with small farmers. It also had to develop a risk management system that drew on information garnered from farmers, customers, and commodities and foreign exchange markets to minimize the risks of crop problems, price and currency volatility, and supply disruption.

These capabilities translated into other contexts. Olam realized that its knowledge of small farmers in Nigeria could be applied to small farmers in, say, Burkina Faso. Its risk management skills could be applied to peanuts or coffee beans as well as to cashews. The company accordingly added both farmers and customers in new countries and new products. It now sources 20 agricultural products from farmers in 65 countries and delivers them to more than 11,000 customers across the world.

Of course, Olam's differentiation evolved as the company grew. For instance, as it expanded into certain countries, it found opportunities to acquire and fold in small operations based in those countries. Although Olam had no experience with M&A, its capabilities and assets, including good contacts at the ground level in its countries of operation, gave it an advantage in recognizing promising opportunities and understanding how to negotiate with and integrate acquisitions.

Over time, the company has developed playbooks for M&A and deal integration and now considers them important differentiating features that frontline managers (and everyone else in the organization) understand and value. As Olam's CEO, Sunny Verghese, explains, "Our line managers find and consummate transactions at the local level. It is sort of a hidden asset that we have because our people are in the market at a lower level of contact than anyone else. Our ability in transactions is now part of our core, and we manage it centrally with a unique repeatable formula of clear rules and criteria."

Supporting Your Differentiation

Although differentiation is at the heart of a repeatable model, it needs the support of a rigorously focused yet flexible organization. Our research shows that powerful differentiations create the most enduring profits when a company delivers them to the front line in the form of simple, nonnegotiable principles and when it creates robust learning systems that facilitate constant adaptation. Let's look at these factors in turn.

Nonnegotiable principles

This is a fundamental building block of repeatability, a way of keeping everyone on the same page. Analysis of our 200-company database reveals that 83% of the best-performing businesses had established explicit, widely understood principles across the organization, while only 26% of the worst performers had done so. Indeed, a link between well-defined, shared core principles and frontline behavior was more highly correlated with business performance than any other factor we studied.

The logic of this connection seems clear. Nonnegotiables translate the most important beliefs and assumptions underlying the company's differentiation into a few prescriptive statements that all employees can understand, relate to, and use as a reference point for making trade-offs and decisions. In effect, they are the headlines of the user's manual for a company's strategy.

To illustrate how companies use nonnegotiables, let's go back to Olam. A key differentiator is that the company manages supply chains right from the farm gate. To support this, Olam requires managers to live in the rural areas of developing countries in order to learn what really goes on at the farms. This nonnegotiable principle is the foundation for hiring criteria, assignments, and the structure and content of training. Another nonnegotiable is that each manager give highest priority to relationships with local farmers. Olam's field operating manual captures many of the routines that support this requirement. The company's principles, and the practices that support them, are central to its culture and provide a bonding experience for managers, who respond to trade-offs and challenges at all levels with remarkable consistency.

Tetra Pak has different but equally powerful nonnegotiables. One of them is that the package must save more than it costs, an idea that originated with the company's founder and was the reason for developing its signature tetrahedron-shaped package for milk or juice. Every major new product, package design, or line of equipment must meet that standard. Tetra Pak has developed sophisticated methods for evaluating the system's cost of packaging, including production costs, spoilage, transportation and storage, and disposal costs. It claims that it can reduce operating costs by as much as 12% for a dairy or juice company.

To understand the power of this consistency, consider that from the moment a business is founded, management becomes increasingly distanced from the customer and the front line. Up and down the organization, information slows and grows distorted—the corporate equivalent of the classic game Telephone, in which a message is relayed around a table in whispers and has become unrecognizable by the time it completes the circuit. When a company internalizes a set of principles, the message no longer gets garbled. A shared point of view, core beliefs, and a common vocabulary improve everyone's ability to communicate and foster self-organization, permitting fewer layers, fewer handoffs, and shorter communication lines. All this increases the speed of a business, which means you can capture more growth opportunities ahead of competitors and accomplish more per unit of time.

Robust learning systems

Clear differentiation supported by nonnegotiables confers a competitive advantage—for a while. As markets shift, however, successful organizations must also be able to learn quickly and adapt to new circumstances. Both our research and the recent history of business reflect the importance of supporting your differentiation with rapid learning and adaptation. Some 48% of managers in our top group of performers felt that their companies were characterized by strong learning systems, compared with only 9% among the rest. The travails of Kodak, General Motors, Xerox, Nokia, Sony, Kmart, and many others can be seen as cases of arrested adaptation—great formulas that simply did not change fast enough. Most such cases, we should note, didn't involve disruptive innovations that caught the incumbent flat-footed. Stalls and stagnation stem from a failure to learn much more often than from a hard-to-predict disruption.

The most common method of learning in companies with great repeatable models comes from direct, immediate customer feedback. The most powerful demonstration we have seen is through Net Promoter systems, which are used at Vanguard, in Apple's retail division, and at many other companies. In this approach, customers are usually asked one or two questions shortly after contact about their satisfaction with the experience and their willingness to recommend the product, service, or company to a friend or colleague. The power of the Net Promoter Score lies in its simplicity.

Companies that chase more-detailed feedback typically find that customers don't bother to engage, so data is fewer and poorer as a result.

In more-complex environments, companies with direct sales forces have other interesting opportunities to create strong feedback loops with customers. Take the toolmaker Hilti. Founded in 1941 by Martin and Eugen Hilti as a mechanical workshop with five employees in Schaan, Liechtenstein, the company focused on innovative tools for difficult construction jobs. Martin Hilti spent much time at job sites, observing and interacting with customers. This was the start of the Hilti direct sales force. Over the decades, the business grew one tool at a time. The company would develop a basic design and then innovate intensively on the details, using information its salespeople acquired at job sites. Today, in an industry where about 75% of products are sold through indirect channels, this direct customer contact remains a differentiated strength. It accounts in part for Hilti's ability to command significant price premiums over competitors.

Real-time response is a competitive weapon of growing importance in a world of increasing speed and complexity. The companies that move fastest can often operate within competitors' decision cycles, so competitors are always responding to them rather than the other way around. Marcia Blenko, Paul Rogers, and Michael Mankins recently studied 760 companies worldwide through 40 questions regarding perceptions of decision speed, quality, and ability to execute. When they synthesized the responses into an index of decision effectiveness, they found that companies ranked in the top quintile produced, on average, a total shareholder return about 6 percentage points higher than the returns of other companies. Companies with robust learning systems usually score higher than average on all three counts.

A repeatable differentiation can falter and even collapse without nonnegotiable principles and robust learning systems—and without strong management to preserve and protect it. Think of Nokia. Its leaders created a formula for tablet-shaped handsets that allowed it to achieve enormous economies of scale and dominate the market for more than a decade. Yet despite considerable surplus resources during that time, the company's leaders failed to adapt and invest aggressively in the future. As a result, in just a year Nokia lost its market position to Apple, Google, and Research In Motion. This lesson is all the more sobering given that Nokia's R&D and product development teams had many years earlier created some of the basic concepts later used in the iPhone: a large display, a touch screen, internet readiness, and an app store.

The search for profitable growth is becoming increasingly difficult. Today fewer than 10% of companies achieve more than a modest level of profitable growth over a decade, and the odds of success are declining. A series of interviews we conducted with CEOs regarding their challenges on the job spotlight two reasons for this state of affairs. One is that companies are forced to adapt faster than ever. The other—and this one was at the top of the list—is the need to control ever-growing levels of complexity. Sluggish, too-complex organizations are the silent killers of corporate growth and profitability. Interestingly, only 15% of executives in our survey cited a lack of attractive opportunities as a major barrier to growth. Internal complexity and barriers to speed of adaptation were far more important.

Our findings show that the simplest strategies, built around the sharpest differentiations, have hidden advantages not only with customers but also internally, with the frontline employees who must mobilize faster and adapt better than competitors. When people in an organization deeply understand the sources of its differentiation, they move in the same direction quickly and effectively, learning and improving the business model as they go. And they turn in remarkable performance year after year.

Originally published in November 2011. Reprint R1111G

Pipelines, Platforms, and the New Rules of Strategy

by Marshall W. Van Alstyne, Geoffrey G. Parker, and Sangeet Paul Choudary

BACK IN 2007 the five major mobile-phone manufacturers—Nokia, Samsung, Motorola, Sony Ericsson, and LG—collectively controlled 90% of the industry's global profits. That year, Apple's iPhone burst onto the scene and began gobbling up market share.

By 2015 the iPhone *single-handedly* generated 92% of global profits, while all but one of the former incumbents made no profit at all.

How can we explain the iPhone's rapid domination of its industry? And how can we explain its competitors' free fall? Nokia and the others had classic strategic advantages that should have protected them: strong product differentiation, trusted brands, leading operating systems, excellent logistics, protective regulation, huge R&D budgets, and massive scale. For the most part, those firms looked stable, profitable, and well entrenched.

Certainly the iPhone had an innovative design and novel capabilities. But in 2007, Apple was a weak, nonthreatening player surrounded by 800-pound gorillas. It had less than 4% of market share in desktop operating systems and none at all in mobile phones.

As we'll explain, Apple (along with Google's competing Android system) overran the incumbents by exploiting the power of platforms and leveraging the new rules of strategy they give rise to. Platform businesses bring together producers and consumers in high-value exchanges. Their chief assets are information and interactions, which together are also the source of the value they create and their competitive advantage.

Understanding this, Apple conceived the iPhone and its operating system as more than a product or a conduit for services. It imagined them as a way to connect participants in two-sided markets—app developers on one side and app users on the other—generating value for both groups. As the number of participants on each side grew, that value increased—a phenomenon called "network effects," which is central to platform strategy. By January 2015 the company's App Store offered 1.4 million apps and had cumulatively generated $25 billion for developers.

Apple's success in building a platform business within a conventional product firm holds critical lessons for companies across industries. Firms that fail to create platforms and don't learn the new rules of strategy will be unable to compete for long.

Pipeline to Platform

Platforms have existed for years. Malls link consumers and merchants; newspapers connect subscribers and advertisers. What's changed in this century is that information technology has profoundly reduced the need to own physical infrastructure and assets. IT makes building and scaling up platforms vastly simpler and cheaper, allows nearly frictionless participation that strengthens network effects, and enhances the ability to capture, analyze, and exchange huge amounts of data that increase the platform's value to all. You don't need to look far to see examples of platform businesses, from Uber to Alibaba to Airbnb, whose spectacular growth abruptly upended their industries.

Though they come in many varieties, platforms all have an ecosystem with the same basic structure, comprising four types of players. The *owners* of platforms control their intellectual property and governance. *Providers* serve as the platforms' interface with users.

Idea in Brief

The Sea Change

Platform businesses that bring together producers and consumers, as Uber and Airbnb do, are gobbling up market share and transforming competition. Traditional businesses that fail to create platforms and to learn the new rules of strategy will struggle.

The New Rules

With a platform, the critical asset is the community and the resources of its members. The focus of strategy shifts from controlling to orchestrating

resources, from optimizing internal processes to facilitating external interactions, and from increasing customer value to maximizing ecosystem value.

The Upshot

In this new world, competition can emerge from seemingly unrelated industries or from within the platform itself. Firms must make smart choices about whom to let onto platforms and what they're allowed to do there, and must track new metrics designed to monitor and boost platform interactions.

Producers create their offerings, and *consumers* use those offerings. (See the exhibit "The players in a platform ecosystem.")

To understand how the rise of platforms is transforming competition, we need to examine how platforms differ from the conventional "pipeline" businesses that have dominated industry for decades. Pipeline businesses create value by controlling a linear series of activities—the classic value-chain model. Inputs at one end of the chain (say, materials from suppliers) undergo a series of steps that transform them into an output that's worth more: the finished product. Apple's handset business is essentially a pipeline. But combine it with the App Store, the marketplace that connects app developers and iPhone owners, and you've got a platform.

As Apple demonstrates, firms needn't be only a pipeline or a platform; they can be both. While plenty of pure pipeline businesses are still highly competitive, when platforms enter the same marketplace, the platforms virtually always win. That's why pipeline giants such as Walmart, Nike, John Deere, and GE are all scrambling to incorporate platforms into their models.

The players in a platform ecosystem

A platform provides the infrastructure and rules for a marketplace that brings together producers and consumers. The players in the ecosystem fill four main roles but may shift rapidly from one role to another. Understanding the relationships both within and outside the ecosystem is central to platform strategy.

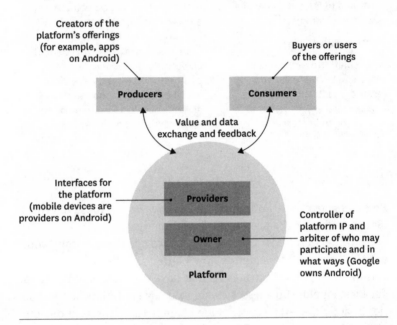

The move from pipeline to platform involves three key shifts:

1. From resource control to resource orchestration. The resource-based view of competition holds that firms gain advantage by controlling scarce and valuable—ideally, inimitable—assets. In a pipeline world, those include tangible assets such as mines and real estate and intangible assets like intellectual property. With platforms, the assets that are hard to copy are the community and the resources its members own and contribute, be they rooms or cars or ideas and information. In other words, the network of producers and consumers is the chief asset.

2. From internal optimization to external interaction. Pipeline firms organize their internal labor and resources to create value by optimizing an entire chain of product activities, from materials sourcing to sales and service. Platforms create value by facilitating interactions between external producers and consumers. Because of this external orientation, they often shed even variable costs of production. The emphasis shifts from dictating processes to persuading participants, and ecosystem governance becomes an essential skill.

3. From a focus on customer value to a focus on ecosystem value. Pipelines seek to maximize the lifetime value of individual customers of products and services, who, in effect, sit at the end of a linear process. By contrast, platforms seek to maximize the total value of an expanding ecosystem in a circular, iterative, feedback-driven process. Sometimes that requires subsidizing one type of consumer in order to attract another type.

These three shifts make clear that competition is more complicated and dynamic in a platform world. The competitive forces described by Michael Porter (the threat of new entrants and substitute products or services, the bargaining power of customers and suppliers, and the intensity of competitive rivalry) still apply. But on platforms these forces behave differently, and new factors come into play. To manage them, executives must pay close attention to the interactions on the platform, participants' access, and new performance metrics.

We'll examine each of these in turn. But first let's look more closely at network effects—the driving force behind every successful platform.

The Power of Network Effects

The engine of the industrial economy was, and remains, supply-side economies of scale. Massive fixed costs and low marginal costs mean that firms achieving higher sales volume than their competitors have a lower average cost of doing business. That allows them to reduce prices, which increases volume further, which permits more price cuts—a virtuous feedback loop that produces monopolies. Supply economics gave us Carnegie Steel, Edison Electric (which became GE), Rockefeller's Standard Oil, and many other industrial era giants.

In supply-side economies, firms achieve market power by controlling resources, ruthlessly increasing efficiency, and fending off challenges from any of the five forces. The goal of strategy in this world is to build a moat around the business that protects it from competition and channels competition toward other firms.

The driving force behind the internet economy, conversely, is demand-side economies of scale, also known as network effects. These are enhanced by technologies that create efficiencies in social networking, demand aggregation, app development, and other phenomena that help networks expand. In the internet economy, firms that achieve higher "volume" than competitors (that is, attract more platform participants) offer a higher average value per transaction. That's because the larger the network, the better the matches between supply and demand and the richer the data that can be used to find matches. Greater scale generates more value, which attracts more participants, which creates more value—another virtuous feedback loop that produces monopolies. Network effects gave us Alibaba, which accounts for over 75% of Chinese e-commerce transactions; Google, which accounts for 82% of mobile operating systems and 94% of mobile search; and Facebook, the world's dominant social platform.

The five forces model doesn't factor in network effects and the value they create. It regards external forces as "depletive," or extracting value from a firm, and so argues for building barriers against them. In demand-side economies, however, external forces can be "accretive"—adding value to the platform business. Thus the power of suppliers and customers, which is threatening in a supply-side world, may be viewed as an asset on platforms. Understanding when external forces may either add or extract value in an ecosystem is central to platform strategy.

How Platforms Change Strategy

In pipeline businesses, the five forces are relatively defined and stable. If you're a cement manufacturer or an airline, your customers and competitive set are fairly well understood, and the boundaries separating your suppliers, customers, and competitors are reasonably clear. In platform businesses, those boundaries can shift rapidly, as we'll discuss.

Forces within the ecosystem

Platform participants—consumers, producers, and providers—typically create value for a business. But they may defect if they believe their needs can be met better elsewhere. More worrisome, they may turn on the platform and compete directly with it. Zynga began as a games producer on Facebook but then sought to migrate players onto its own platform. Amazon and Samsung, providers of devices for the Android platform, tried to create their own versions of the operating system and take consumers with them.

The new roles that players assume can be either accretive or depletive. For example, consumers and producers can swap roles in ways that generate value for the platform. Users can ride with Uber today and drive for it tomorrow; travelers can stay with Airbnb one night and serve as hosts for other customers the next. In contrast, providers on a platform may become depletive, especially if they decide to compete with the owner. Netflix, a provider on the platforms of telecommunication firms, has control of consumers' interactions with the content it offers, so it can extract value from the platform owners while continuing to rely on their infrastructure.

As a consequence, platform firms must constantly encourage accretive activity within their ecosystems while monitoring participants' activity that may prove depletive. This is a delicate governance challenge that we'll discuss further.

Forces exerted by ecosystems

Managers of pipeline businesses can fail to anticipate platform competition from seemingly unrelated industries. Yet successful platform businesses tend to move aggressively into new terrain

Networks Invert the Firm

PIPELINE FIRMS HAVE LONG outsourced aspects of their internal functions, such as customer service. But today companies are taking that shift even further, moving toward orchestrating external networks that can complement or entirely replace the activities of once-internal functions.

Inversion extends outsourcing: Where firms might once have furnished design specifications to a known supplier, they now tap ideas they haven't yet imagined from third parties they don't even know. Firms are being turned inside out as value-creating activities move beyond their direct control and their organizational boundaries.

Marketing is no longer just about creating internally managed outbound messages. It now extends to the creation and propagation of messages by consumers themselves. Travel destination marketers invite consumers to submit videos of their trips and promote them on social media. The online eyeglasses retailer Warby Parker encourages consumers to post online photos of themselves modeling different styles and ask friends to help them choose. Consumers get more-flattering glasses, and Warby Parker gets viral exposure.

Information technology, historically focused on managing internal enterprise systems, increasingly supports external social and community networks. Threadless, a producer of T-shirts, coordinates communication not just to and from but among customers, who collaborate to develop the best product designs.

---

and into what were once considered separate industries with little warning. Google has moved from web search into mapping, mobile operating systems, home automation, driverless cars, and voice recognition. As a result of such shape-shifting, a platform can abruptly transform an incumbent's set of competitors. Swatch knows how to compete with Timex on watches but now must also compete with Apple. Siemens knows how to compete with Honeywell in thermostats but now is being challenged by Google's Nest.

Competitive threats tend to follow one of three patterns. First, they may come from an established platform with superior network effects that uses its relationships with customers to enter your industry. Products have features; platforms have communities, and those communities can be leveraged. Given Google's relation-

Human resources functions at companies increasingly leverage the wisdom of networks to augment internal talent. Enterprise software giant SAP has opened the internal system on which its developers exchange problems and solutions to its external ecosystem—to developers at both its own partners and its partners' clients. Information sharing across this network has improved product development and productivity and reduced support costs.

Finance, which historically has recorded its activities on private internal accounts, now records some transactions externally on public, or "distributed," ledgers. Organizations such as IBM, Intel, and JPMorgan are adopting blockchain technology that allows ledgers to be securely shared and vetted by anyone with permission. Participants can inspect everything from aggregated accounts to individual transactions. This allows firms to, for example, crowdsource compliance with accounting principles or seek input on their financial management from a broad network outside the company. Opening the books this way taps the wisdom of crowds and signals trustworthiness.

Operations and logistics traditionally emphasize the management of just-in-time inventory. More and more often, that function is being supplanted by the management of "not even mine" inventory—whether rooms, apps, or other assets owned by network participants. Indeed, if Marriott, Yellow Cab, and NBC had added platforms to their pipeline value chains, then Airbnb, Uber, and YouTube might never have come into being.

ship with consumers, the value its network provides them, and its interest in the internet of things, Siemens might have predicted the tech giant's entry into the home-automation market (though not necessarily into thermostats). Second, a competitor may target an overlapping customer base with a distinctive new offering that leverages network effects. Airbnb's and Uber's challenges to the hotel and taxi industries fall into this category. The final pattern, in which platforms that collect the same type of data that your firm does suddenly go after your market, is still emerging. When a data set is valuable, but different parties control different chunks of it, competition between unlikely camps may ensue. This is happening in health care, where traditional providers, producers of wearables like Fitbit, and retail pharmacies like Walgreens are all launching platforms based on the health data they own. They can be expected to compete for control of a broader data set—and the consumer relationships that come with it.

Focus

Managers of pipeline businesses focus on growing sales. For them, goods and services delivered (and the revenues and profits from them) are the units of analysis. For platforms, the focus shifts to interactions—exchanges of value between producers and consumers on the platform. The unit of exchange (say, a view of a video or a thumbs-up on a post) can be so small that little or no money changes hands. Nevertheless, the number of interactions and the associated network effects are the ultimate source of competitive advantage.

With platforms, a critical strategic aim is strong up-front design that will attract the desired participants, enable the right interactions (so-called core interactions), and encourage ever-more-powerful network effects. In our experience, managers often fumble here by focusing too much on the wrong type of interaction. And the perhaps counterintuitive bottom line, given how much we stress the importance of network effects, is that it's usually wise to ensure the value of interactions for participants before focusing on volume.

Most successful platforms launch with a single type of interaction that generates high value even if, at first, low volume. They then move into adjacent markets or adjacent types of interactions, increasing both value and volume. Facebook, for example, launched with a narrow focus (connecting Harvard students to other Harvard students) and then opened the platform to college students broadly and ultimately to everyone. LinkedIn launched as a professional networking site and later entered new markets with recruitment, publishing, and other offerings.

Access and governance

In a pipeline world, strategy revolves around erecting barriers. With platforms, while guarding against threats remains critical, the focus of strategy shifts to eliminating barriers to production and consumption in order to maximize value creation. To that end,

Harnessing Spillovers

POSITIVE SPILLOVER EFFECTS help platforms rapidly increase the volume of interactions. Book purchases on a platform, for example, generate book recommendations that create value for other participants on it, who then buy more books. This dynamic exploits the fact that network effects are often strongest among interactions of the same type (say, book sales) than among unrelated interactions (say, package pickup and yardwork in different cities mediated by the odd-job platform TaskRabbit).

Consider ride sharing. By itself, an individual ride on Uber is high value for both rider and driver—a desirable core interaction. As the number of platform participants increases, so does the value Uber delivers to both sides of the market; it becomes easier for consumers to get rides and for drivers to find fares. Spillover effects further enhance the value of Uber to participants: Data from riders' interactions with drivers—ratings of drivers and riders—improves the value of the platform to other users. Similarly, data on how well a given ride matched a rider's needs helps determine optimal pricing across the platform—another important spillover effect.

platform executives must make smart choices about access (whom to let onto the platform) and governance (or "control"—what consumers, producers, providers, and even competitors are allowed to do there).

Platforms consist of rules and architecture. Their owners need to decide how open both should be. An *open architecture* allows players to access platform resources, such as app developer tools, and create new sources of value. *Open governance* allows players other than the owner to shape the rules of trade and reward sharing on the platform. Regardless of who sets the rules, a fair reward system is key. If managers open the architecture but do not share the rewards, potential platform participants (such as app developers) have the ability to engage but no incentives. If managers open the rules and rewards but keep the architecture relatively closed, potential participants have incentives to engage but not the ability.

These choices aren't fixed. Platforms often launch with a fairly closed architecture and governance and then open up as they introduce new types of interactions and sources of value. But every platform must induce producers and consumers to interact and share their ideas and resources. Effective governance will inspire outsiders to bring valuable intellectual property to the platform, as Zynga did in bringing FarmVille to Facebook. That won't happen if prospective partners fear exploitation.

Some platforms encourage producers to create high-value offerings on them by establishing a policy of "permissionless innovation." They let producers invent things for the platform without approval but guarantee the producers will share in the value created. Rovio, for example, didn't need permission to create the Angry Birds game on the Apple operating system and could be confident that Apple wouldn't steal its IP. The result was a hit that generated enormous value for all participants on the platform. However, Google's Android platform has allowed even more innovation to flourish by being more open at the provider layer. That decision is one reason Google's market capitalization surpassed Apple's in early 2016 (just as Microsoft's did in the 1980s).

However, unfettered access can destroy value by creating "noise"—misbehavior or excess or low-quality content that inhibits interaction. One company that ran into this problem was Chatroulette, which paired random people from around the world for webchats. It grew exponentially until noise caused its abrupt collapse. Initially utterly open—it had no access rules at all—it soon encountered the "naked hairy man" problem, which is exactly what it sounds like. Clothed users abandoned the platform in droves. Chatroulette responded by reducing its openness with a variety of user filters.

Most successful platforms similarly manage openness to maximize positive network effects. Airbnb and Uber rate and insure hosts and drivers, Twitter and Facebook provide users with tools to prevent stalking, and Apple's App Store and the Google Play store both filter out low-quality applications.

Metrics

Leaders of pipeline enterprises have long focused on a narrow set of metrics that capture the health of their businesses. For example, pipelines grow by optimizing processes and opening bottlenecks;

one standard metric, inventory turnover, tracks the flow of goods and services through them. Push enough goods through and get margins high enough, and you'll see a reasonable rate of return.

As pipelines launch platforms, however, the numbers to watch change. Monitoring and boosting the performance of core interactions becomes critical. Here are new metrics managers need to track:

Interaction failure. If a traveler opens the Lyft app and sees "no cars available," the platform has failed to match an intent to consume with supply. Failures like these directly diminish network effects. Passengers who see this message too often will stop using Lyft, leading to higher driver downtimes, which can cause drivers to quit Lyft, resulting in even lower ride availability. Feedback loops can strengthen or weaken a platform.

Engagement. Healthy platforms track the participation of ecosystem members that enhances network effects—activities such as content sharing and repeat visits. Facebook, for example, watches the ratio of daily to monthly users to gauge the effectiveness of its efforts to increase engagement.

Match quality. Poor matches between the needs of users and producers weaken network effects. Google constantly monitors users' clicking and reading to refine how its search results fill their requests.

Negative network effects. Badly managed platforms often suffer from other kinds of problems that create negative feedback loops and reduce value. For example, congestion caused by unconstrained network growth can discourage participation. So can misbehavior, as Chatroulette found. Managers must watch for negative network effects and use governance tools to stem them by, for example, withholding privileges or banishing troublemakers.

Finally, platforms must understand the financial value of their communities and their network effects. Consider that in 2016, private equity markets placed the value of Uber, a demand economy firm founded in 2009, above that of GM, a supply economy firm founded in 1908. Clearly Uber's investors were looking beyond the traditional financials and metrics when calculating the firm's worth and potential. This is a clear indication that the rules have changed.

Because platforms require new approaches to strategy, they also demand new leadership styles. The skills it takes to tightly control internal resources just don't apply to the job of nurturing external ecosystems.

While pure platforms naturally launch with an external orientation, traditional pipeline firms must develop new core competencies—and a new mind-set—to design, govern, and nimbly expand platforms on top of their existing businesses. The inability to make this leap explains why some traditional business leaders with impressive track records falter in platforms. Media mogul Rupert Murdoch bought the social network Myspace and managed it the way he might have run a newspaper—from the top down, bureaucratically, and with a focus more on controlling the internal operation than on fostering the ecosystem and creating value for participants. In time the Myspace community dissipated and the platform withered.

The failure to transition to a new approach explains the precarious situation that traditional businesses—from hotels to health care providers to taxis—find themselves in. For pipeline firms, the writing is on the wall: Learn the new rules of strategy for a platform world, or begin planning your exit.

Originally published in April 2016. Reprint R1604C

Why the Lean Start-Up Changes Everything

by Steve Blank

LAUNCHING A NEW ENTERPRISE—whether it's a tech start-up, a small business, or an initiative within a large corporation—has always been a hit-or-miss proposition. According to the decades-old formula, you write a business plan, pitch it to investors, assemble a team, introduce a product, and start selling as hard as you can. And somewhere in this sequence of events, you'll probably suffer a fatal setback. The odds are not with you: As new research by Harvard Business School's Shikhar Ghosh shows, 75% of all start-ups fail.

But recently an important countervailing force has emerged, one that can make the process of starting a company less risky. It's a methodology called the "lean start-up," and it favors experimentation over elaborate planning, customer feedback over intuition, and iterative design over traditional "big design up front" development. Although the methodology is just a few years old, its concepts—such as "minimum viable product" and "pivoting"—have quickly taken root in the start-up world, and business schools have already begun adapting their curricula to teach them.

The lean start-up movement hasn't gone totally mainstream, however, and we have yet to feel its full impact. In many ways it is roughly where the big data movement was five years ago—consisting mainly of a buzzword that's not yet widely understood, whose implications companies are just beginning to grasp. But as its practices spread, they're turning the conventional wisdom about entrepreneurship on its head. New ventures of all kinds are attempting to improve their chances of success by following its principles of failing fast and continually learning. And despite the methodology's name, in the long term some of its biggest payoffs may be gained by the *large* companies that embrace it.

In this article I'll offer a brief overview of lean start-up techniques and how they've evolved. Most important, I'll explain how, in combination with other business trends, they could ignite a new entrepreneurial economy.

The Fallacy of the Perfect Business Plan

According to conventional wisdom, the first thing every founder must do is create a business plan—a static document that describes the size of an opportunity, the problem to be solved, and the solution that the new venture will provide. Typically it includes a five-year forecast for income, profits, and cash flow. A business plan is essentially a research exercise written in isolation at a desk before an entrepreneur has even begun to build a product. The assumption is that it's possible to figure out most of the unknowns of a business in advance, before you raise money and actually execute the idea.

Once an entrepreneur with a convincing business plan obtains money from investors, he or she begins developing the product in a similarly insular fashion. Developers invest thousands of man-hours to get it ready for launch, with little if any customer input. Only after building and launching the product does the venture get substantial feedback from customers—when the sales force attempts to sell it. And too often, after months or even years of development, entrepreneurs learn the hard way that customers do not need or want most of the product's features.

After decades of watching thousands of start-ups follow this standard regimen, we've now learned at least three things:

1. Business plans rarely survive first contact with customers. As the boxer Mike Tyson once said about his opponents' prefight strategies: "Everybody has a plan until they get punched in the mouth."

Idea in Brief

Over the past few years, a new methodology for launching companies, called the "lean start-up," has begun to replace the old regimen.

Instead of executing business plans, operating in stealth mode, and releasing fully functional prototypes, young ventures are testing hypotheses, gathering early and frequent customer feedback, and showing "minimum viable products" to prospects. This new process recognizes that searching for a business model (which is the primary task facing a start-up) is entirely different from executing against that model (which is what established firms do).

Recently, business schools have begun to teach the methodology, which can also be learned at events such as Startup Weekend. Over time, lean start-up techniques could reduce the failure rate of new ventures and, in combination with other trends taking hold in the business world, launch a new, more entrepreneurial economy.

2. No one besides venture capitalists and the late Soviet Union requires five-year plans to forecast complete unknowns. These plans are generally fiction, and dreaming them up is almost always a waste of time.

3. Start-ups are not smaller versions of large companies. They do not unfold in accordance with master plans. The ones that ultimately succeed go quickly from failure to failure, all the while adapting, iterating on, and improving their initial ideas as they continually learn from customers.

One of the critical differences is that while existing companies *execute* a business model, start-ups *look* for one. This distinction is at the heart of the lean start-up approach. It shapes the lean definition of a start-up: a temporary organization designed to search for a repeatable and scalable business model.

The lean method has three key principles:

First, rather than engaging in months of planning and research, entrepreneurs accept that all they have on day one is a series of untested hypotheses—basically, good guesses. So instead of writing an intricate business plan, founders summarize their hypotheses in

Sketch out your hypotheses

The business model canvas lets you look at all nine building blocks of your business on one page. Each component of the business model contains a series of hypotheses that you need to test.

Key partners	Key activities	Value propositions	Customer relationships	Customer segments
Who are our key partners? Who are our key suppliers? Which key resources are we acquiring from our partners? Which key activities do partners perform?	What key activities do our value propositions require? Our distribution channels? Customer relationships? Revenue streams?	What value do we deliver to the customer? Which one of our customers' problems are we helping to solve? What bundles of products and services are we offering to each segment? Which customer needs are we satisfying? What is the minimum viable product?	How do we get, keep, and grow customers? Which customer relationships have we established? How are they integrated with the rest of our business model? How costly are they?	For whom are we creating value? Who are our most important customers? What are the customer archetypes?
	Key resources		**Channels**	
	What key resources do our value propositions require? Our distribution channels? Customer relationships? Revenue streams?		Through which channels do our customer segments want to be reached? How do other companies reach them now? Which ones work best? Which ones are most cost-efficient? How are we integrating them with customer routines?	

Cost structure		Revenue streams	
What are the most important costs inherent to our business model? Which key resources are most expensive? Which key activities are most expensive?		For what value are our customers really willing to pay? For what do they currently pay? What is the revenue model? What are the pricing tactics?	

Source: www.businessmodelgeneration.com/canvas. Canvas concept developed by Alexander Osterwalder and Yves Pigneur.

a framework called a *business model canvas*. Essentially, this is a diagram of how a company creates value for itself and its customers. (See the exhibit "Sketch out your hypotheses.")

Second, lean start-ups use a "get out of the building" approach called *customer development* to test their hypotheses. They go out and ask potential users, purchasers, and partners for feedback on all elements of the business model, including product features, pricing, distribution channels, and affordable customer acquisition strategies. The emphasis is on nimbleness and speed: New ventures rapidly assemble minimum viable products and immediately elicit customer feedback. Then, using customers' input to revise their assumptions, they start the cycle over again, testing redesigned offerings and making further small adjustments (iterations) or more substantive ones (pivots) to ideas that aren't working. (See the exhibit "Listen to customers.")

Third, lean start-ups practice something called *agile development,* which originated in the software industry. Agile development works hand-in-hand with customer development. Unlike typical yearlong product development cycles that presuppose knowledge of customers' problems and product needs, agile development eliminates wasted time and resources by developing the product iteratively and incrementally. It's the process by which start-ups create the minimum viable products they test. (See the exhibit "Quick, responsive development.")

When Jorge Heraud and Lee Redden started Blue River Technology, they were students in my class at Stanford. They had a vision of building robotic lawn mowers for commercial spaces. After talking to over 100 customers in 10 weeks, they learned their initial customer target—golf courses—didn't value their solution. But then they began to talk to farmers and found a huge demand for an automated way to kill weeds without chemicals. Filling it became their new product focus, and within 10 weeks Blue River had built and tested a prototype. Nine months later the start-up had obtained more than $3 million in venture funding. The team expected to have a commercial product ready just nine months after that.

Listen to customers

During customer development, a start-up searches for a business model that works. If customer feedback reveals that its business hypotheses are wrong, it either revises them or "pivots" to new hypotheses. Once a model is proven, the start-up starts executing, building a formal organization. Each stage of customer development is iterative: A start-up will probably fail several times before finding the right approach.

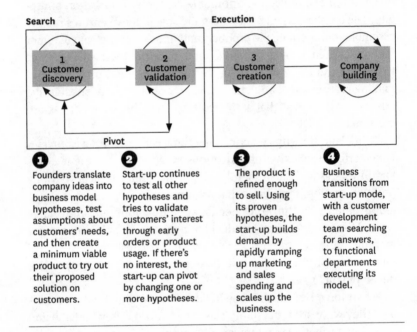

Search   Execution

1 Customer discovery → 2 Customer validation → 3 Customer creation → 4 Company building

Pivot

1 Founders translate company ideas into business model hypotheses, test assumptions about customers' needs, and then create a minimum viable product to try out their proposed solution on customers.

2 Start-up continues to test all other hypotheses and tries to validate customers' interest through early orders or product usage. If there's no interest, the start-up can pivot by changing one or more hypotheses.

3 The product is refined enough to sell. Using its proven hypotheses, the start-up builds demand by rapidly ramping up marketing and sales spending and scales up the business.

4 Business transitions from start-up mode, with a customer development team searching for answers, to functional departments executing its model.

Stealth Mode's Declining Popularity

Lean methods are changing the language start-ups use to describe their work. During the dot-com boom, start-ups often operated in "stealth mode" (to avoid alerting potential competitors to a market opportunity), exposing prototypes to customers only during highly orchestrated "beta" tests. The lean start-up methodology makes those concepts obsolete because it holds that in most industries customer feedback matters more than secrecy and that constant feedback yields better results than cadenced unveilings.

Those two fundamental precepts crystallized for me during my career as an entrepreneur. (I've been involved with eight high-tech start-ups, as either a founder or an early employee.) When I shifted into teaching, a decade ago, I came up with the formula for customer development described earlier. By 2003 I was outlining this process in a course at the Haas School of Business at the University of California at Berkeley.

In 2004, I invested in a start-up founded by Eric Ries and Will Harvey and, as a condition of my investment, insisted that they take my course. Eric quickly recognized that waterfall development, the tech industry's traditional, linear product development approach, should be replaced by iterative agile techniques. He also saw similarities between this emerging set of start-up disciplines and the Toyota Production System, which had become known as "lean manufacturing." Eric dubbed the combination of customer development and agile practices the "lean start-up."

The tools were popularized by a series of successful books. In 2003, I wrote *The Four Steps to the Epiphany,* articulating for the first time that start-ups were not smaller versions of large companies and laying out the customer development process in detail. In 2010, Alexander Osterwalder and Yves Pigneur gave entrepreneurs the standard framework for business model canvases in *Business Model Generation.* In 2011 Eric published an overview in *The Lean Startup.* And in 2012 Bob Dorf and I summarized what we'd learned about lean techniques in a step-by-step handbook called *The Startup Owner's Manual.*

The lean start-up method is now being taught at more than 25 universities and through a popular online course at Udacity.com. In addition, in almost every city around world, you'll find organizations like Startup Weekend introducing the lean method to hundreds of prospective entrepreneurs at a time. At such gatherings a roomful of start-up teams can cycle through half a dozen potential product ideas in a matter of hours. Although it sounds incredible to people who haven't been to one, at these events some businesses are formed on a Friday evening and are generating actual revenue by Sunday afternoon.

Quick, responsive development

In contrast to traditional product development, in which each stage occurs in linear order and lasts for months, agile development builds products in short, repeated cycles. A start-up produces a "minimum viable product"—containing only critical features—gathers feedback on it from customers, and then starts over with a revised minimum viable product.

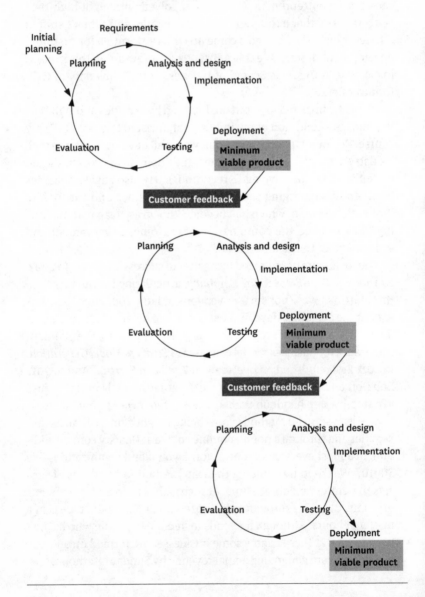

Creating an Entrepreneurial, Innovation-Based Economy

While some adherents claim that the lean process can make individual start-ups more successful, I believe that claim is too grandiose. Success is predicated on too many factors for one methodology to guarantee that any single start-up will be a winner. But on the basis of what I've seen at hundreds of start-ups, at programs that teach lean principles, and at established companies that practice them, I can make a more important claim: Using lean methods across a portfolio of start-ups will result in fewer failures than using traditional methods.

A lower start-up failure rate could have profound economic consequences. Today the forces of disruption, globalization, and regulation are buffeting the economies of every country. Established industries are rapidly shedding jobs, many of which will never return. Employment growth in the 21st century will have to come from new ventures, so we all have a vested interest in fostering an environment that helps them succeed, grow, and hire more workers. The creation of an innovation economy that's driven by the rapid expansion of start-ups has never been more imperative.

In the past, growth in the number of start-ups was constrained by five factors in addition to the failure rate:

1. The high cost of getting the first customer and the even higher cost of getting the product wrong

2. Long technology development cycles

3. The limited number of people with an appetite for the risks inherent in founding or working at a start-up

4. The structure of the venture capital industry, in which a small number of firms each needed to invest big sums in a handful of start-ups to have a chance at significant returns

5. The concentration of real expertise in how to build start-ups, which in the United States was mostly found in pockets on the East and West coasts (This is less an issue in Europe and other parts of the world, but even overseas there are geographic entrepreneurial hot spots.)

What Lean Start-Ups Do Differently

THE FOUNDERS OF LEAN START-UPS don't begin with a business plan; they begin with the search for a business model. Only after quick rounds of experimentation and feedback reveal a model that works do lean founders focus on execution.

Lean	Traditional
STRATEGY	
Business model Hypothesis-driven	**Business plan** Implementation-driven
NEW-PRODUCT PROCESS	
Customer development Get out of the office and test hypotheses	**Product management** Prepare offering for market following a linear, step-by-step plan
ENGINEERING	
Agile development Build the product iteratively and incrementally	**Agile or waterfall development** Build the product iteratively, or fully specify the product before building it
ORGANIZATION	
Customer and agile development teams Hire for learning, nimbleness, and speed	**Departments by function** Hire for experience and ability to execute
FINANCIAL REPORTING	
Metrics that matter Customer acquisition cost, lifetime customer value, churn, viralness	**Accounting** Income statement, balance sheet, cash flow statement
FAILURE	
Expected Fix by iterating on ideas and pivoting away from ones that don't work	**Exception** Fix by firing executives
SPEED	
Rapid Operates on good-enough data	**Measured** Operates on complete data

The lean approach reduces the first two constraints by helping new ventures launch products that customers actually want, far more quickly and cheaply than traditional methods, and the third by making start-ups less risky. And it has emerged at a time when other business and technology trends are likewise breaking down the barriers to start-up formation. The combination of all these forces is altering the entrepreneurial landscape.

Today open source software, like GitHub, and cloud services, such as Amazon Web Services, have slashed the cost of software development from millions of dollars to thousands. Hardware start-ups no longer have to build their own factories, since offshore manufacturers are so easily accessible. Indeed, it's become quite common to see young tech companies that practice the lean start-up methodology offer software products that are simply "bits" delivered over the web or hardware that's built in China within weeks of being formed. Consider Roominate, a start-up designed to inspire girls' confidence and interest in science, technology, engineering, and math. Once its founders had finished testing and iterating on the design of their wired dollhouse kit, they sent the specs off to a contract manufacturer in China. Three weeks later the first products arrived.

Another important trend is the decentralization of access to financing. Venture capital used to be a tight club of formal firms clustered near Silicon Valley, Boston, and New York. In today's entrepreneurial ecosystem, new super angel funds, smaller than the traditional hundred-million-dollar-sized VC fund, can make early-stage investments. Worldwide, hundreds of accelerators, like Y Combinator and TechStars, have begun to formalize seed investments. And crowdsourcing sites like Kickstarter provide another, more democratic method of financing start-ups.

The instantaneous availability of information is also a boon to today's new ventures. Before the internet, new company founders got advice only as often as they could have coffee with experienced investors or entrepreneurs. Today the biggest challenge is sorting through the overwhelming amount of start-up advice they get. The lean concepts provide a framework that helps you differentiate the good from the bad.

Lean start-up techniques were initially designed to create fast-growing tech ventures. But I believe the concepts are equally valid for creating the Main Street small businesses that make up the bulk of the economy. If the entire universe of small business embraced them, I strongly suspect it would increase growth and efficiency, and have a direct and immediate impact on GDP and employment.

There are signs that this may in fact happen. In 2011 the U.S. National Science Foundation began using lean methods to commercialize basic science research in a program called the Innovation Corps. Eleven universities now teach the methods to hundreds of teams of senior research scientists across the United States.

MBA programs are adopting these techniques, too. For years they taught students to apply large-company approaches—such as accounting methods for tracking revenue and cash flow, and organizational theories about managing—to start-ups. Yet start-ups face completely different issues. Now business schools are realizing that new ventures need their own management tools.

As business schools embrace the distinction between management execution and searching for a business model, they're abandoning the business plan as the template for entrepreneurial education. And the business plan competitions that have been a celebrated part of the MBA experience for over a decade are being replaced by business model competitions. (Harvard Business School became the latest to make this switch, in 2012.) Stanford, Harvard, Berkeley, and Columbia are leading the charge and embracing the lean start-up curriculum. My Lean LaunchPad course for educators is now training over 250 college and university instructors a year.

A New Strategy for the 21st-Century Corporation

It's already becoming clear that lean start-up practices are not just for young tech ventures.

Corporations have spent the past 20 years increasing their efficiency by driving down costs. But simply focusing on improving existing business models is not enough anymore. Almost every large company understands that it also needs to deal with ever-increasing external threats by continually innovating. To ensure their survival and growth, corporations need to keep inventing new business models. This challenge requires entirely new organizational structures and skills.

Over the years managerial experts such as Clayton Christensen, Rita McGrath, Vijay Govindarajan, Henry Chesbrough, Ian MacMillan, Alexander Osterwalder, and Eric von Hippel have advanced the thinking on how large companies can improve their innovation processes. During the past three years, however, we have seen large companies, including General Electric, Qualcomm, and Intuit, begin to implement the lean start-up methodology.

GE's Energy Storage division, for instance, is using the approach to transform the way it innovates. In 2010 Prescott Logan, the general manager of the division, recognized that a new battery developed by the unit had the potential to disrupt the industry. Instead of preparing to build a factory, scale up production, and launch the new offering (ultimately named Durathon) as a traditional product extension, Logan applied lean techniques. He started searching for a business model and engaging in customer discovery. He and his team met face-to-face with dozens of global prospects to explore potential new markets and applications. These weren't sales calls: The team members left their PowerPoint slides behind and listened to customers' issues and frustrations with the battery status quo. They dug deep to learn how customers bought industrial batteries, how often they used them, and the operating conditions. With this feedback, they made a major shift in their customer focus. They eliminated one of their initial target segments, data centers, and discovered a new one—utilities. In addition, they narrowed the broad customer segment of "telecom" to cell phone providers in developing countries with unreliable electric grids. Eventually GE invested $100 million to build a world-class battery manufacturing facility in Schenectady, New York, which it opened in 2012. According to press reports, demand for the new batteries is so high that GE is already running a backlog of orders.

The first hundred years of management education focused on building strategies and tools that formalized execution and efficiency for existing businesses. Now, we have the first set of tools for searching for new business models as we launch start-up ventures. It also happens to have arrived just in time to help existing companies deal with the forces of continual disruption. In the 21st century those forces will make people in every kind of organization—start-ups, small businesses, corporations, and government—feel the pressure of rapid change. The lean start-up approach will help them meet it head-on, innovate rapidly, and transform business as we know it.

Originally published in May 2013. Reprint R1305C

Strategy Needs Creativity

by Adam Brandenburger

I'VE NOTICED THAT BUSINESS SCHOOL STUDENTS often feel frustrated when they're taught strategy. There's a gap between what they learn and what they'd like to learn. Strategy professors (including me) typically teach students to think about strategy problems by introducing them to rigorous analytical tools—assessing the five forces, drawing a value net, plotting competitive positions. The students know that the tools are essential, and they dutifully learn how to use them. But they also realize that the tools are better suited to understanding an existing business context than to dreaming up ways to reshape it. Game-changing strategies, they know, are born of creative thinking: a spark of intuition, a connection between different ways of thinking, a leap into the unexpected.

They're right to feel this way—which is not to say that we should abandon the many powerful analytical tools we've developed over the years. We'll always need them to understand competitive landscapes and to assess how companies can best deploy their resources and competencies there. But we who devote our professional lives to thinking about strategy need to acknowledge that just giving people those tools will not help them break with conventional ways of thinking. If we want to teach students—and executives—how to generate groundbreaking strategies, we must give them tools explicitly designed to foster creativity.

A number of such tools already exist, often in practitioner-friendly forms. In "How Strategists Really Think: Tapping the Power of Analogy" (HBR, April 2005), Giovanni Gavetti and Jan W. Rivkin write compellingly about using analogies to come up with new business models. Charles Duhigg talks in his book *Smarter Faster Better* about introducing carefully chosen creative "disturbances" into work processes to spur new thinking. Youngme Moon, in "Break Free from the Product Life Cycle" (HBR, May 2005), suggests redefining products by boldly limiting—rather than augmenting—the features offered.

What these approaches have in common is the goal of moving strategy past the insights delivered by analytic tools (which are close at hand) and into territory that's further afield, or—to use a bit of academic jargon—*cognitively distant*. They take their inspiration more from how our thought processes work than from how industries or business models are structured. For that reason they can help strategists make the creative leap beyond what already exists to invent a genuinely new way of doing business. Simply waiting for inspiration to strike is not the answer.

In this article I explore four approaches to building a breakthrough strategy:

- **Contrast.** The strategist should identify—and challenge—the assumptions undergirding the company's or the industry's status quo. This is the most direct and often the most powerful way to reinvent a business.

- **Combination.** Steve Jobs famously said that creativity is "just connecting things"; many smart business moves come from linking products or services that seem independent from or even in tension with one another.

- **Constraint.** A good strategist looks at an organization's limitations and considers how they might actually become strengths.

- **Context.** If you reflect on how a problem similar to yours was solved in an entirely different context, surprising insights

Idea in Brief

The Problem

The field of strategy overfocuses on analytic rigor and underfocuses on creativity.

Why It Matters

Analytic tools are good at helping strategists develop business ideas that are close at hand—but less

good at discovering transformative strategies.

In Practice

The wise strategist can work with four creativity-enhancing tools: contrast, combination, constraint, and context.

may emerge. (I wrote about these ideas more academically in "Where Do Great Strategies Really Come From?" *Strategy Science,* December 2017.)

These approaches aren't exhaustive—or even entirely distinct from one another—but I've found that they help people explore a wide range of possibilities.

Contrast: What Pieces of Conventional Wisdom Are Ripe for Contradiction?

To create a strategy built on contrast, first identify the assumptions implicit in existing strategies. Elon Musk seems to have a knack for this approach. He and the other creators of PayPal took a widely held but untested assumption about banking—that transferring money online was feasible and safe between institutions but not between individuals—and disproved it. With SpaceX he is attempting to overturn major assumptions about space travel: that it must occur on a fixed schedule, be paid for by the public, and use onetime rockets. He may be on track toward a privately funded, on-demand business that reuses rockets.

It's best to be precise—even literal—when naming such assumptions. Consider the video rental industry in 2000. Blockbuster ruled the industry, and the assumptions beneath its model seemed self-evident: People pick up videos at a retail location close to home. Inventory must be limited because new videos are expensive. Since the demand for them is high, customers must be charged for late returns. (It was basically a public-library model.) But Netflix put those assumptions under a microscope. Why is a physical location necessary? Mailing out videos would be cheaper and more convenient. Is there a way around the high fees for new releases? If the studios were open to a revenue-sharing agreement, both parties could benefit. Those two changes allowed Netflix to carry lots more movies, offer long rental periods, do away with late fees—and remake an industry.

Most of the time, strategy from contrast may look less revolutionary than Netflix (which remade itself again by streaming videos and becoming a content creator) or SpaceX (should it succeed). Any organization can ask whether it might usefully flip the order in which it performs activities, for example. The traditional model in retail is to start with a flagship store (usually in a city center) and add satellites (in suburban locations). Now consider pop-up stores: In some cases they conform to the old model—they are like mini-satellites; but in others the pop-up comes first, and if that's successful, a larger footprint is added. The Soho area of New York City has become a testing ground for this strategy.

Another approach is to consider shaking up the value chain, which in any industry is conventionally oriented in a particular way, with some players acting as suppliers and others as customers. Inverting the value chain may yield new business models. In the charitable sector, for example, donors have been seen as suppliers of financial resources. DonorsChoose.org is a model that treats them more like customers. The organization puts up a "storefront" of requests posted by schoolteachers around the United States who are looking for materials for their (often underresourced) classrooms. Donors can choose which requests to respond to and receive photos of the schoolwork that their money has supported. In effect, they are buying the satisfaction of seeing a particular classroom before and after.

In some industries the status quo has dictated highly bundled, expensive products or services. Unbundling them is another way to build a contrast strategy. Various segments of the market may prefer to get differing subsets of the bundle at better prices. Challengers' unbundling of the status quo has been facilitated by the internet in one industry after another: Music, TV, and education are leading examples. Incumbents have to make major internal changes to compete with unbundlers, rendering this approach especially effective.

How to begin
1. Precisely identify the assumptions that underlie conventional thinking in your company or industry.

2. Think about what might be gained by proving one or more of them false.

3. Deliberately disturb an aspect of your normal work pattern to break up ingrained assumptions.

What to watch out for
Because the assumptions underlying your business model are embedded in all your processes—and because stable businesses need predictability—it won't be easy to change course. Organizations are very good at resisting change.

Combination: How Can You Connect Products or Services That Have Traditionally Been Separate?

Combination is a canonical creative approach in both the arts and the sciences. As Anthony Brandt and David Eagleman note in *The Runaway Species,* it was by combining two very different ideas—a ride in an elevator and a journey into space—that Albert Einstein found his way to the theory of general relativity. In business, too, creative and successful moves can result from combining things that have been separate. Often these opportunities arise with complementary products and services. Products and payment systems, for example, have traditionally been separate nodes in value chains. But the Chinese social media platform WeChat (owned by Tencent) now includes an integrated mobile payment platform called WeChat Pay that enables users to buy and sell products within their social networks. Expanding beyond the Chinese ecosystem, Tencent and Alibaba are coordinating with overseas payment firms to enable retailers in other countries to accept their mobile payment services.

Sometimes competitors can benefit from joining forces to grow the pie. (Barry Nalebuff and I explored this idea in our 1996 book *Co-opetition*.) For example, BMW and Daimler have announced plans to combine their mobility services—car sharing, ride hailing, car parking, electric vehicle charging, and tickets for public transport. Presumably, the two automakers hope that this move will be an effective counterattack against Uber and other players that are encroaching on the traditional car industry.

In other instances, companies from wholly separate industries have created new value for customers by combining offerings. Apple and Nike have done so since the 2006 introduction of the Nike+ iPod Sport Kit, which enabled Nike shoes to communicate with an iPod for tracking steps. More recently, versions of the Apple Watch have come with the Nike+ Run Club app fully integrated. Nest Labs and Amazon also complement each other: Nest's intelligent home thermostat becomes even more valuable when it can deploy voice control via Amazon's virtual assistant, Alexa.

New technologies are a rich source of combinatorial possibilities. AI and blockchain come together naturally to protect the privacy of the large amounts of personal data needed to train algorithms in health care and other sensitive areas. Blockchain and the internet of things come together in the form of sensors and secure data in decentralized applications such as food supply chains, transportation systems, and smart homes, with automated insurance included in smart contracts.

Perhaps the biggest combination today is the one emerging between humans and machines. Some commentators see the future of that relationship as more competitive than cooperative, with humans losing out in many areas of economic life. Others predict a more positive picture, in which machines take on lower-level cognition, freeing humans to be more creative. Martin Reeves and Daichi Ueda have written about algorithms that allow companies to make frequent, calibrated adjustments to their business models, enabling humans to work on high-level objectives and think beyond the present. (See "Designing the Machines That Will Design Strategy," HBR.org, April 2016.)

Strategy from combination involves looking for connections across traditional boundaries, whether by linking a product and a service, two technologies, the upstream and the downstream, or other ingredients. Here, too, the creative strategist must challenge the status quo—this time by thinking not just outside the box but across two or more boxes.

How to begin

1. Form groups with diverse expertise and experience; brainstorm new combinations of products and services.

2. Look for ways to coordinate with providers of complementary products (who may even be competitors).

What to watch out for

Businesses often manage for and measure profits at the individual product or activity level. But combinations require system-level thinking and measurements.

Constraint: How Can You Turn Limitations or Liabilities into Opportunities?

The world's first science fiction story, *Frankenstein,* was written when its author, Mary Wollstonecraft Shelley, was staying near Lake Geneva during an unusually cold and stormy summer and found herself trapped indoors with nothing to do but exercise her imagination. Artists know a lot about constraints—from profound ones, such as serious setbacks in their lives, to structural ones, such as writing a 14-line poem with a specified rhyming structure. In business, too, creative thinking turns limitations into opportunities.

That constraints can spark creative strategies may seem paradoxical. Lift a constraint, and any action that was previously possible is surely still possible; most likely, more is now possible.

But that misses the point that one can think multiple ways in a given situation—and a constraint may prompt a whole new line of thinking. Of course, the Goldilocks principle applies: Too many constraints will choke off all possibilities, and a complete absence of constraints is a problem too.

Tesla hasn't lacked financial resources in entering the car industry, but it doesn't have a traditional dealership network (considered a key part of automakers' business models) through which to sell. Rather than get into the business of building one, Tesla has chosen to sell cars online and to build Apple-like stores staffed with salespeople on salary. This actually positions the company well relative to competitors, whose dealers may be conflicted about promoting electric vehicles over internal-combustion ones. In addition, Tesla controls its pricing directly, whereas consumers who buy electric vehicles from traditional dealers may encounter significant variations in price.

I should note that this attitude toward constraints is very different from that suggested by the classic SWOT analysis. Strategists are supposed to identify the strengths, weaknesses, opportunities, and threats impinging on an organization and then figure out ways to exploit strengths and opportunities and mitigate weaknesses and threats.

In stark contrast, a constraint-based search would look at how those weaknesses could be turned to the company's advantage. Constraint plus imagination may yield an opportunity.

This approach to strategy turns the SWOT tool upside down in another way as well. Just as an apparent weakness can be turned into a strength, an apparent strength can prove to be a weakness. The likelihood of this often increases over time, as the assets that originally enabled a business to succeed become liabilities when the environment changes. For example, big retailers have historically considered "success" to be moving product out the door; to that end, they needed large physical footprints with on-site inventory. Among the many changes they face today is the rise of "guideshops"—a term used by the menswear retailer Bonobos—where shoppers try on items, which they can have shipped to them or later order online. In the new environment, traditional retail footprints become more of a liability than an asset.

Another way to approach strategy from constraint is to ask whether you might benefit from self-imposed constraints. (Artists do something similar when they choose to work only within a particular medium.) The famous Copenhagen restaurant Noma adheres to the New Nordic Food manifesto (emphasizing purity, simplicity, beauty, seasonality, local tradition, and innovation). A similar strategy of working only with local suppliers has been adopted by thousands of restaurants around the world. A commitment to high environmental standards, fair labor practices, and ethical supply-chain management can be powerful for organizations looking to lead change in their industries or sectors.

Self-imposed constraints can also spur innovation. Adam Morgan and Mark Barden, in their book *A Beautiful Constraint*, describe the efforts of the Audi racing team in the early 2000s to win Le Mans under the assumption that its cars couldn't go faster than the competition's. Audi developed diesel-powered racers, which required fewer fuel stops than gasoline-powered cars, and won Le Mans three years in succession (2004–2006). In 2017 Audi set itself a new constraint—and a new ambition: to build winning all-electric racers for the new Formula E championship.

How to begin

1. List the "incompetencies" (rather than the competencies) of your organization—and test whether they can in fact be turned into strengths.

2. Consider deliberately imposing some constraints to encourage people to find new ways of thinking and acting.

What to watch out for

Successful businesses face few obvious constraints; people may feel no need to explore how new ones might create new opportunities.

Context: How Can Far-Flung Industries, Ideas, or Disciplines Shed Light on Your Most Pressing Problems?

An entire field, biomimetics, is devoted to finding solutions in nature to problems that arise in engineering, materials science, medicine, and elsewhere. For example, the burrs from the burdock plant, which propagate by attaching to the fur of animals via tiny hooks, inspired George de Mestral in the 1940s to create a clothing fastener that does not jam (as zippers are prone to do). Thus the invention of Velcro. This is a classic problem-solving technique. Start with a problem in one context, find another context in which an analogous problem has already been solved, and import the solution.

Intel did that when it came up with its famous Intel Inside logo, in the early 1990s. The goal was to turn Intel microprocessors into a branded product to speed up consumers' adoption of next-generation chips and, more broadly, to improve the company's ability to drive the PC industry forward. Branded ingredients were well established in certain consumer product sectors—examples include Teflon and NutraSweet—but hadn't been tried in the world of technology. Intel imported the approach to high tech with a novel advertising campaign, successfully branding what had previously been an invisible computer component.

Context switching can be done across industries, as in Intel's case, or even across time. The development of the graphical user interface (GUI) for computers was in a sense the result of a step backward: The developers moved from immersion in the text-based context in which programming had grown up to thinking about the highly visual hand-eye environment in which young children operate. Similarly, some AI researchers are currently looking at how children learn in order to inform processes for machine learning.

Companies are always eager to see into the future, of course, and techniques for trying to do so are well established. That is the purpose of lead-user and extreme-user innovation strategies, which ask companies to shift their attention from mainstream customers to people who are designing their own versions or using products in unexpected ways in especially demanding environments. Information about where the edges of the market are today can signal where the mainstream will be tomorrow. Extreme sports, such as mountain biking, skateboarding, snowboarding, and windsurfing, are good examples. In an MIT Sloan School working paper, Sonali Shah relates that aficionados led many of the innovations in those areas, starting in the 1950s, and big manufacturers added cost efficiencies and marketing to take them mainstream.

When companies locate R&D functions far from headquarters, they're acknowledging the importance of jumping into someone else's context. This is not just a strategy for large companies that move people to Silicon Valley for tech or the Boston area for biotech. Start-ups, too, should put themselves in the best context for learning and growth. The hardware accelerator HAX, located in Shenzhen, hosts hardware start-up teams from numerous countries and enables them to tap into the high-speed ecosystem of the "hardware capital of the world," quadrupling the rate at which they cycle through iterations of their prototypes.

Strategy focused on context may involve transferring a solution from one setting to another more or less as is. It may mean uncovering entirely new thinking about problems (or opportunities) by finding pioneers who are ahead of the game. At bottom, it's about not being trapped in a single narrative.

How to begin

1. Explain your business to an outsider in another industry. Fresh eyes from a different context can help uncover new answers and opportunities.

2. Engage with lead users, extreme users, and innovation hotspots.

What to watch out for

Businesses need to focus on internal processes to deliver on their current value propositions—but the pressure to focus internally can get in the way of learning from the different contexts in which other players operate.

In the world of management consulting, aspects of "strategy" and "innovation" have started to converge. IDEO, the design and innovation powerhouse, has moved into strategy consulting, for example—while McKinsey has added design-thinking methods to its strategy consulting. This convergence raises an obvious question: If the distinction between strategy and innovation is less clear than it once was, do we really need to think carefully about the role of creativity in the strategy-making process?

I believe strongly that the answer is yes. At its core, strategy is still about finding ways to create and claim value through differentiation. That's a complicated, difficult job. To be sure, it requires tools that can help identify surprising, creative breaks from conventional thinking. But it also requires tools for analyzing the competitive landscape, the dynamics threatening that landscape, and a company's resources and competencies. We need to teach business school students—and executives—how to be creative and rigorous at the same time.

Originally published in March–April 2019. Reprint R1902C

Put Purpose at the Core of Your Strategy

by Thomas W. Malnight, Ivy Buche, and Charles Dhanaraj

2019

EIGHT YEARS AGO we launched a global study of high growth in companies, investigating the importance of three strategies known to drive it: creating new markets, serving broader stakeholder needs, and changing the rules of the game. What we found surprised us. Although each of those approaches did boost growth at the organizations we studied, there was a fourth driver we hadn't considered at all: *purpose.*

Companies have long been encouraged to build purpose into what they do. But usually it's talked about as an add-on—a way to create shared value, improve employee morale and commitment, give back to the community, and help the environment. But as we worked with the high-growth companies in our study and beyond, we began to recognize that many of them had moved purpose from the periphery of their strategy to its core—where, with committed leadership and financial investment, they had used it to generate sustained profitable growth, stay relevant in a rapidly changing world, and deepen ties with their stakeholders.

Two Critical Roles

In the course of our research, we talked to scores of C-level executives. They worked at 28 companies—in the United States, Europe, and India—that had had an average compound annual growth rate of

30% or more in the previous five years. What we learned from those conversations was that purpose played two important strategic roles: It helped companies *redefine the playing field,* and it allowed them to *reshape the value proposition.* And that, in turn, enabled them to overcome the challenges of slowing growth and declining profitability.

Role 1: Redefining the playing field

What's a key difference between low-growth and high-growth companies? The former spend most of their time fighting for market share on one playing field, which naturally restricts their growth potential. And because most aggressive battles take place in industries that are slowing down, gains in market share come at a high cost, often eroding profits and competitive advantage as offerings become commoditized.

High-growth companies, by contrast, don't feel limited to their current playing field. Instead, they think about whole ecosystems, where connected interests and relationships among multiple stakeholders create more opportunities. But these firms don't approach ecosystems haphazardly. They let purpose be their guide.

Consider the different strategies adopted by the two leading companies in the pet-food industry: Nestlé Purina PetCare, the largest player in North America; and Mars Petcare, the global leader. The companies have defined very similar purposes for themselves—"Better with pets" (Purina) and "A better world for pets" (Mars Petcare)—and both want to develop new products that will help customers improve their pets' health. But Purina has continued to focus on the pet-food playing field and is applying purpose in some inspiring social initiatives, whereas Mars Petcare is using purpose to propel its expansion in the broader field of pet health.

Mars Petcare, which had established a foothold in pet health with the acquisition of Banfield Pet Hospital in 2007, decided to build its presence in that arena by buying two other veterinary services: Blue-Pearl in 2015 and VCA in 2017. Then in 2018 Mars Petcare entered the European veterinary market, buying the Swedish company AniCura, which has operations in seven European countries, and the British

Idea in Brief

The Challenge

Companies pursuing high growth tend to follow three well-known strategies: creating new markets, serving broader stakeholder needs, and changing the rules of the game. But there's another critical growth driver: purpose.

The Insight

Many companies consider purpose merely an add-on to their strategy, but the most successful companies put it at the core, using it to redefine the playing field and reshape their value propositions.

The Benefits

A purpose-driven strategy helps companies overcome the challenges of slowing growth and declining profits. It also helps with the soft side of management: the people-related aspects of running a business, which so often prove to be the undoing of leaders.

company Linnaeus. Those acquisitions helped Mars Petcare become Mars Inc.'s largest and fastest-growing business division.

In moving deeper into this larger ecosystem, Mars Petcare did more than just capitalize on a burgeoning industry. It also shifted its orientation beyond products to services, a radical change for an asset-heavy company that for 75 years had relied on the production and sale of goods. To succeed, the company had to build completely different core competencies and devise a new organizational structure. Many companies in this dangerously open-ended situation might have flailed, but Mars Petcare did not. It was able to pull off a transformation because it ensured that every move it made was aligned with the same core purpose. And it's not done yet: The company is now bringing that sense of purpose to efforts to expand into pet-activity monitoring with "smart" collars.

Another company that has used purpose to redefine the playing field, this time in the industrial sector, is the Finnish oil-refining firm Neste. For more than six decades Neste, founded in 1948, operated a business focused almost entirely on crude oil, but by 2009 it was struggling. The market was glutted, oil prices had dropped sharply, margins were falling, and the EU had passed new carbon-emissions legislation. During the previous two years the company's market value had shrunk by 50%.

Fighting those headwinds, the executive team, led by Neste's new CEO, Matti Lievonen, realized that the company could no longer survive on its traditional playing field. It would have to look for new opportunities in the larger ecosystem. Renewable energy could be a key driver of growth, they realized. Their purpose, they decided, should be to develop sustainable sources of energy that would help reduce emissions, and everything they did would be guided by a simple idea: "Creating responsible choices every day."

It's common for major oil companies to nod to sustainability in some way, but Lievonen quickly proved that Neste meant business, launching a bold transformation that would become a seven-year journey. Employees, customers, and investors all initially resisted the change, but Lievonen and his team were undaunted. They made major investments in infrastructure, innovated renewable technologies, focused on converting customers to green energy solutions, and, most important, engineered a fundamental change in the company's culture.

The process wasn't easy. When Lievonen was just three months into his tenure, a leading economic magazine in Finland published an article saying that he should be fired. He soldiered on, however, and by 2015 Neste had established itself as the world's largest producer of renewable fuels derived from waste and residues. A year later its comparable operating profits from renewables would surpass those of its oil-products business. In 2017 the company took yet another step by actively researching and promoting the use of waste feedstock from new sources such as algae oil, microbial oil, and tall oil pitch.

Role 2: Reshaping the value proposition

When confronted with eroding margins in a rapidly commodifying world, companies often enhance their value propositions by innovating products, services, or business models. That can bring some quick wins, but it's a transactional approach geared toward prevailing in the current arena. Because a purpose-driven approach facilitates growth in new ecosystems, it allows companies to broaden their mission, create a holistic value proposition, and deliver lifetime benefits to customers.

Companies can make this shift in three main ways: by responding to trends, building on trust, and focusing on pain points.

Responding to trends. In line with its purpose of "contributing to a safer society," Sweden's Securitas AB, a security company with 370,000 employees, has traditionally offered physical guarding services. But in the early 2010s its CEO at the time, Alf Göransson, saw that globalization, urbanization, and the increasingly networked business landscape were all changing the nature of risk—for people, operations, and business continuity. At the same time, labor was becoming more expensive, and new technologies were becoming cheaper. Given those developments, Göransson decided that Securitas could no longer "simply sell man-hours." Instead, the company had to explore new ways of using electronics to provide security. This shift, Göransson understood, was not a threat to the existing business but an opportunity to grow—as indeed it has proved to be.

In 2018 the company decided to go a step further and reshape its value proposition from reactive to predictive security, a plan that once again built on the company's core purpose. Under the leadership of Göransson's successor, Magnus Ahlqvist, the firm strengthened its electronic security business by acquiring a number of companies, investing heavily in modernizing and integrating back-office systems, and training its guards in remote surveillance, digital reporting, and efficient response. That allowed Securitas to offer bundled, customized security solutions—encompassing physical guarding, electronic security, and risk management—that provided a much-enhanced level of protection at an optimized cost. By expanding its value proposition in this way, Securitas has been able to strengthen client relationships and significantly increase its margins for the solutions business. From 2012 to 2018 the company's sales of security solutions and electronic security also increased, from 6% of total revenue to 20%.

Building on trust. When Mahindra Finance, the financial services arm of the Mahindra Group, a $20 billion Indian conglomerate, wanted to define its value proposition, it looked to its parent company's longtime purpose-driven strategy of improving customers' lives—encapsulated in 2010 by the simple motto "Rise." It's a word that the company's third-generation leader, Anand Mahindra, expects will inspire employees to accept no limits, think alternatively, and drive positive change.

In keeping with that strategy, Mahindra Finance decided to target its core offering, vehicle financing, to rural areas, where it could—as Rajeev Dubey, the group head of HR, put it to us—"address the unmet needs of underserved customers in an underpenetrated market."

That meant that the company had to figure out how to determine the creditworthiness of customers who were mostly poor, illiterate, and unbanked, with no identity documents, no collateral, and cash flows that were often impacted by monsoons. To do that, the company had to develop completely new ways to handle loan design, repayment terms, customer approval, branch locations, and disbursement and collection in cash. Not only that, but it had to figure out how to recruit workers who could speak local dialects, assess local situations, and operate under a decentralized model of decision making.

Remarkably, the company managed to do all those things and established a preliminary level of trust with its customers. It then stretched its value proposition to help farmers and other customers obtain insurance for their tractors, lives, and health. In a country where insurance penetration is abysmally low (about 3.5%), this was no small feat, especially since rural residents didn't easily part with any minuscule monthly surplus they had, even if it was to secure their livelihood.

Then Mahindra Finance extended its purpose-driven efforts to housing finance, another arena in which it recognized that it could help its rural customers rise above their circumstances. For most of those people, securing loans for housing was difficult in the extreme. Banks offered loans at an interest rate of about 10% but demanded

Is Purpose at the Core of Your Strategy?

NOT UNLESS you answer yes to all five questions below.

	Y	N
1. Does purpose contribute to increasing your company's growth and profitability today?	❏	❏
2. Does purpose significantly influence your strategic decisions and investment choices?	❏	❏
3. Does purpose shape your core value proposition?	❏	❏
4. Does purpose affect how you build and manage your organizational capabilities?	❏	❏
5. Is purpose on the agenda of your leadership team every time you meet?	❏	❏

documentation most rural residents couldn't provide. Moneylenders offered instant financing but charged interest rates of about 40%. Recognizing an opportunity, Mahindra Finance decided to play at the intermediate level, offering customized home loans at rates of about 14%, an option that appealed to its growing base of customers. And when some of those customers developed successful small agribusinesses, they began looking for working-capital loans, equipment loans, project finance, and so on—more unmet needs that Mahindra Finance could address. So it extended its value proposition again, into the small-to-medium-enterprise arena, offering finance and asset-management services.

Throughout its expansion, Mahindra Finance was guided by its goal of helping rural citizens improve their lives. The company identified and committed itself to value propositions that allowed it to deepen its relationship with its customers, which in turn created additional streams of revenue and profits. Today Mahindra Finance is India's largest rural nonbanking financial company, serving 50% of villages and 6 million customers.

Focusing on pain points. We've already seen how Mars Petcare's health care value proposition led to direct connections with pet owners at multiple touchpoints. Having established them, the company looked for other ways to create "a better world for pets." How could it come up with a value proposition that would make pet ownership a seamless, convenient, and attractive experience?

The answer was by investing in technology to help address one of the biggest concerns of pet owners: *preventing* health problems. In 2016 the company acquired Whistle, the San Francisco–based maker of a connected collar for activity monitoring and location tracking—a kind of Fitbit for dogs. Teaming the device up with its Banfield Pet Hospital unit, the company launched the Pet Insight Project, a three-year longitudinal study that aims to enroll 200,000 dogs in the United States. By combining machine learning, data science, and deep veterinary expertise, the project seeks to understand when behavior may signal a change in a pet's health and how owners can partner with their veterinarians on individualized diagnostics and treatments for their pets.

Developing a Purpose

Leaders and companies that have effectively defined corporate purpose typically have done so with one of two approaches: *retrospective* or *prospective*.

The retrospective approach builds on a firm's existing reason for being. It requires that you look back, codify organizational and cultural DNA, and make sense of the firm's past. The focus of the discovery process is internal. Where have we come from? How did we get here? What makes us unique to all stakeholders? Where does our DNA open up future opportunities we believe in? These are the kinds of questions leaders have to ask.

Anand Mahindra very successfully employed this tactic at the Mahindra Group. First he looked back at his 30 years at the company and at the values that had guided him as its leader. Then he delved into the psyche of the organization by conducting internal surveys of managers at all levels. He also did ethnographic research in seven countries to identify themes that resonated with his company's multinational, cross-cultural employee base. The process took three years, but ultimately Mahindra arrived at "Rise," which, he realized, had been fundamental to the company from its inception. "'Rise' is not a clever tagline," he has said. "We were already living and operating this way."

The prospective approach, on the other hand, reshapes your reason for being. It requires you to look forward, take stock of the broader ecosystem in which you want to work, and assess your potential for impact in it. The idea is to make sense of the future and then start gearing your organization for it. The focus is external, and leaders have to ask a different set of questions: Where can we go? Which trends affect our business? What new needs, opportunities, and challenges lie ahead? What role can we play that will open up future opportunities for ourselves that we believe in?

The prospective approach can be particularly useful for new CEOs. In 2018, when Magnus Ahlqvist took charge at Securitas, he spearheaded a "purpose workstream" to capture aspirations for the company from the ground up. He asked all his business-unit leaders to run "listening workshops" (with groups of employees from diverse functions, levels, age groups, genders, and backgrounds), which were held over six months. At the end of that period, the findings were collated and analyzed. Among the discoveries: Employees had a vision of transforming the company from a *service provider* to a *trusted adviser*. That shift would require anticipating and responding to security issues instead of relying on the legacy methods of observing and reporting. So employee input helped executives refine the firm's predictive-security strategy.

Implementing a Purpose-Driven Strategy

Our research shows that a compelling purpose clarifies what a company stands for, provides an impetus for action, and is aspirational. But some purpose statements are so generic that they could apply to any company (like Nissan's, "Enriching people's lives"), while others provide only a narrow description of the company's existing businesses (like Wells Fargo's, "We want to satisfy our customers' financial needs and help them succeed financially"). Even if organizations do manage to define their purpose well, they often don't properly translate it into action—or do anything at all to fulfill it. In those cases the purpose becomes nothing more than nice-sounding words on a wall.

Leaders need to think hard about how to make purpose central to their strategy. The two best tactics for doing that are to *transform the leadership agenda* and to *disseminate purpose throughout the organization.*

Consider Mars Petcare again. In 2015 its president, Poul Weihrauch, significantly altered the composition and focus of the leadership team. Its new collective agenda, he declared, would go beyond the performance of individual businesses; it would include generating "multiplier effects" among the businesses (such as between pet food and pet health) and increasing their contributions to creating a better world for pets.

In keeping with that principle, Weihrauch had the company adopt an "outside-in" approach to meeting stakeholder needs. As part of this effort, in 2018 Mars Petcare launched two new programs to support start-ups innovating in pet care: Leap Venture Studio, a business accelerator formed in partnership with Michelson Found Animals and R/GA; and Companion Fund, a $100 million venture-capital fund in partnership with Digitalis Ventures. In announcing these initiatives the company declared that its ambition was "to become a partner of choice for everyone willing to change the rules of the game in pet care."

Revising a leadership agenda and restructuring an organization are arguably easier at a privately held company like Mars Petcare than at a publicly held one. But Finland's Neste is public, with a major stake held by the government, and it has managed to do both things very effectively.

Neste faced an uphill battle when it decided to move into renewables. The company had to build new capabilities while confronting strong opposition from many employees who didn't buy into the change in direction. About 10% of them left during the first year of the strategy's implementation. Painful as it was, it proved to be a positive development, since the company could not have forged ahead with people who didn't believe in its new purpose.

And forge ahead it did. Neste put in place a new top management team, mobilized its 1,500 R&D engineers, innovated patented renewable technology, and invested €2 billion in building new refineries.

The shift also raised a big question for Neste. How could it change its organizational mind-set from *volume* to *value* selling—which entailed convincing customers that its clean fuels would be better for them in the long run? That shift meant going beyond wholesalers to work directly with the distributors and even the distributors' customers. The new leadership team realized that a much higher level of collaboration among business segments and functions was imperative. Winning deals was no longer the sole responsibility of the sales department. The expertise of the whole organization—product knowledge, marketing, finance, taxation—would be required to understand the specific needs of customers like airlines and bus fleets. So Neste engineered a major reorganization and created a matrix structure, in the process rotating about 25% of senior managers and about 50% of upper professionals into new positions. Targets and incentive plans became cross-functional, designed to build capabilities both within and across businesses. And at every step, purpose helped everybody in the company understand the "why" (the business environment's increasing emphasis on sustainability), the "what" (value-creation programs offering renewable solutions to customers, which in turn generated higher margins for Neste), and the "how" (changing from a sales organization to a key-account management model with dedicated people responsible for strategic customers).

The process worked. Neste is now a leader in the renewables industry, and the world is starting to pay attention. In 2015, for example, Google and UPS began partnering with the company to reduce their carbon emissions, as did several cities in California, among them San Francisco and Oakland. In 2018, *Forbes* ranked Neste second on its Global 100 list of the world's most-sustainable companies.

Benefits on the Soft Side

Purpose can also help with the soft side of management—the people-related aspects of running a business, which so often prove to be the undoing of leaders. By putting purpose at the core of strategy, firms can realize three specific benefits: more-unified organizations, more-motivated stakeholders, and a broader positive impact on society.

Unifying the organization

When companies pursue dramatic change and move into larger ecosystems, as both Mars Petcare and Securitas have done, it's unsettling for employees. Why does a pet-food company need to develop a platform to support technology start-ups? Why does an on-site guarding company want to provide electronic security services that could, over time, make the physical presence of guards redundant? Purpose helps employees understand the whys and get on board with the new direction.

Motivating stakeholders

According to the Edelman trust barometer, distrust of government, businesses, the media, and NGOs is now pervasive. At the same time, more than ever, employees, especially Millennials, want to work for organizations that can be trusted to contribute to a higher cause. And when customers, suppliers, and other stakeholders see that a company has a strong higher purpose, they are more likely to trust it and more motivated to interact with it.

Broadening impact

Strategy involves exploring some fundamental questions. Why are we in this business? What value can we bring? What role does my unit play within the bigger portfolio? Purpose creates a basis for answering those questions and defining how each unit will contribute to the organization and to society as a whole. This focus on collective objectives, in turn, opens up many more opportunities to improve growth and profitability today and in the future.

The approach to purpose that we're recommending cannot be a one-off effort. Leaders need to constantly assess how purpose can guide strategy, and they need to be willing to adjust or redefine this relationship as conditions change. That demands a new kind of sustained focus, but the advantages it can confer are legion.

Originally published in September–October 2019. Reprint R1905D

Creating Shared Value

by Michael E. Porter and Mark R. Kramer

THE CAPITALIST SYSTEM is under siege. In recent years business increasingly has been viewed as a major cause of social, environmental, and economic problems. Companies are widely perceived to be prospering at the expense of the broader community.

Even worse, the more business has begun to embrace corporate responsibility, the more it has been blamed for society's failures. The legitimacy of business has fallen to levels not seen in recent history. This diminished trust in business leads political leaders to set policies that undermine competitiveness and sap economic growth. Business is caught in a vicious circle.

A big part of the problem lies with companies themselves, which remain trapped in an outdated approach to value creation that has emerged over the past few decades. They continue to view value creation narrowly, optimizing short-term financial performance in a bubble while missing the most important customer needs and ignoring the broader influences that determine their longer-term success. How else could companies overlook the well-being of their customers, the depletion of natural resources vital to their businesses, the viability of key suppliers, or the economic distress of the communities in which they produce and sell? How else could companies think that simply shifting activities to locations with ever lower wages was a sustainable "solution" to competitive challenges? Government and civil society have often exacerbated the problem by attempting to address social weaknesses at the expense of business. The presumed trade-offs between economic efficiency and social progress have been institutionalized in decades of policy choices.

Companies must take the lead in bringing business and society back together. The recognition is there among sophisticated business and thought leaders, and promising elements of a new model are emerging. Yet we still lack an overall framework for guiding these efforts, and most companies remain stuck in a "social responsibility" mind-set in which societal issues are at the periphery, not the core.

The solution lies in the principle of shared value, which involves creating economic value in a way that *also* creates value for society by addressing its needs and challenges. Businesses must reconnect company success with social progress. Shared value is not social responsibility, philanthropy, or even sustainability, but a new way to achieve economic success. It is not on the margin of what companies do but at the center. We believe that it can give rise to the next major transformation of business thinking.

A growing number of companies known for their hard-nosed approach to business—such as GE, Google, IBM, Intel, Johnson & Johnson, Nestlé, Unilever, and Walmart—have already embarked on important efforts to create shared value by reconceiving the intersection between society and corporate performance. Yet our recognition of the transformative power of shared value is still in its genesis. Realizing it will require leaders and managers to develop new skills and knowledge—such as a far deeper appreciation of societal needs, a greater understanding of the true bases of company productivity, and the ability to collaborate across profit/nonprofit boundaries. And government must learn how to regulate in ways that enable shared value rather than work against it.

Capitalism is an unparalleled vehicle for meeting human needs, improving efficiency, creating jobs, and building wealth. But a narrow conception of capitalism has prevented business from harnessing its full potential to meet society's broader challenges. The opportunities have been there all along but have been overlooked. Businesses acting as businesses, not as charitable donors, are the most powerful force for addressing the pressing issues we face. The

Idea in Brief

The concept of shared value—which focuses on the connections between societal and economic progress—has the power to unleash the next wave of global growth.

An increasing number of companies known for their hard-nosed approach to business—such as Google, IBM, Intel, Johnson & Johnson, Nestlé, Unilever, and Walmart—have begun to embark on important shared value initiatives. But our understanding of the potential of shared value is just beginning.

There are three key ways that companies can create shared value opportunities:

- By reconceiving products and markets

- By redefining productivity in the value chain

- By enabling local cluster development

Every firm should look at decisions and opportunities through the lens of shared value. This will lead to new approaches that generate greater innovation and growth for companies—and also greater benefits for society.

moment for a new conception of capitalism is now; society's needs are large and growing, while customers, employees, and a new generation of young people are asking business to step up.

The purpose of the corporation must be redefined as creating shared value, not just profit per se. This will drive the next wave of innovation and productivity growth in the global economy. It will also reshape capitalism and its relationship to society. Perhaps most important of all, learning how to create shared value is our best chance to legitimize business again.

Moving Beyond Trade-Offs

Business and society have been pitted against each other for too long. That is in part because economists have legitimized the idea that to provide societal benefits, companies must temper their economic success. In neoclassical thinking, a requirement for social improvement—such as safety or hiring the disabled—imposes a constraint on the corporation. Adding a constraint to a firm that is already maximizing profits, says the theory, will inevitably raise costs and reduce those profits.

A related concept, with the same conclusion, is the notion of externalities. Externalities arise when firms create social costs that they do not have to bear, such as pollution. Thus, society must impose taxes, regulations, and penalties so that firms "internalize" these externalities—a belief influencing many government policy decisions.

This perspective has also shaped the strategies of firms themselves, which have largely excluded social and environmental considerations from their economic thinking. Firms have taken the broader context in which they do business as a given and resisted regulatory standards as invariably contrary to their interests. Solving social problems has been ceded to governments and to NGOs. Corporate responsibility programs—a reaction to external pressure—have emerged largely to improve firms' reputations and are treated as a necessary expense. Anything more is seen by many as an irresponsible use of shareholders' money. Governments, for their part, have often regulated in a way that makes shared value more difficult to achieve. Implicitly, each side has assumed that the other is an obstacle to pursuing its goals and acted accordingly.

The concept of shared value, in contrast, recognizes that societal needs, not just conventional economic needs, define markets. It also recognizes that social harms or weaknesses frequently create *internal* costs for firms—such as wasted energy or raw materials, costly accidents, and the need for remedial training to compensate for inadequacies in education. And addressing societal harms and constraints does not necessarily raise costs for firms, because they can innovate through using new technologies, operating methods, and management approaches—and as a result, increase their productivity and expand their markets.

Shared value, then, is not about personal values. Nor is it about "sharing" the value already created by firms—a redistribution approach. Instead, it is about expanding the total pool of economic and social value. A good example of this difference in perspective is the fair trade movement in purchasing. Fair trade aims to increase the proportion of revenue that goes to poor farmers by paying them higher prices for the same crops. Though this may be a noble sentiment, fair trade is mostly about redistribution rather than expanding the overall amount of value created. A shared value perspective, instead, focuses on improving growing techniques and strengthening the local cluster of supporting suppliers and other institutions in order to increase farmers' efficiency, yields, product quality, and sustainability. This leads to a bigger pie of revenue and profits that benefits both farmers and the companies that buy from them. Early studies of cocoa farmers in the Côte d'Ivoire, for instance, suggest that while fair trade can increase farmers' incomes by 10% to 20%, shared value investments can raise their incomes by more than 300%. Initial investment and time may be required to implement new procurement practices and develop the supporting cluster, but the return will be greater economic value and broader strategic benefits for all participants.

The Roots of Shared Value

At a very basic level, the competitiveness of a company and the health of the communities around it are closely intertwined. A business needs a successful community, not only to create demand for its products but also to provide critical public assets and a supportive environment. A community needs successful businesses to provide jobs and wealth creation opportunities for its citizens. This interdependence means that public policies that undermine the productivity and competitiveness of businesses are self-defeating, especially in a global economy where facilities and jobs can easily move elsewhere. NGOs and governments have not always appreciated this connection.

In the old, narrow view of capitalism, business contributes to society by making a profit, which supports employment, wages, purchases, investments, and taxes. Conducting business as usual is sufficient social benefit. A firm is largely a self-contained entity, and social or community issues fall outside its proper scope. (This is the argument advanced persuasively by Milton Friedman in his critique of the whole notion of corporate social responsibility.)

What Is "Shared Value"?

THE CONCEPT OF SHARED VALUE can be defined as policies and operating practices that enhance the competitiveness of a company while simultaneously advancing the economic and social conditions in the communities in which it operates. Shared value creation focuses on identifying and expanding the connections between societal and economic progress.

The concept rests on the premise that both economic and social progress must be addressed using value principles. Value is defined as benefits relative to costs, not just benefits alone. Value creation is an idea that has long been recognized in business, where profit is revenues earned from customers minus the costs incurred. However, businesses have rarely approached societal issues from a value perspective but have treated them as peripheral matters. This has obscured the connections between economic and social concerns.

In the social sector, thinking in value terms is even less common. Social organizations and government entities often see success solely in terms of the benefits achieved or the money expended. As governments and NGOs begin to think more in value terms, their interest in collaborating with business will inevitably grow.

This perspective has permeated management thinking for the past two decades. Firms focused on enticing consumers to buy more and more of their products. Facing growing competition and shorter-term performance pressures from shareholders, managers resorted to waves of restructuring, personnel reductions, and relocation to lower-cost regions, while leveraging balance sheets to return capital to investors. The results were often commoditization, price competition, little true innovation, slow organic growth, and no clear competitive advantage.

In this kind of competition, the communities in which companies operate perceive little benefit even as profits rise. Instead, they perceive that profits come at their expense, an impression that has become even stronger in the current economic recovery, in which rising earnings have done little to offset high unemployment, local business distress, and severe pressures on community services.

It was not always this way. The best companies once took on a broad range of roles in meeting the needs of workers, communities, and supporting businesses. As other social institutions appeared on the scene, however, these roles fell away or were delegated. Shortening investor time horizons began to narrow thinking about appropriate investments. As the vertically integrated firm gave way to greater reliance on outside vendors, outsourcing and offshoring weakened the connection between firms and their communities. As firms moved disparate activities to more and more locations, they often lost touch with any location. Indeed, many companies no longer recognize a home—but see themselves as "global" companies.

These transformations drove major progress in economic efficiency. However, something profoundly important was lost in the process, as more-fundamental opportunities for value creation were missed. The scope of strategic thinking contracted.

Strategy theory holds that to be successful, a company must create a distinctive value proposition that meets the needs of a chosen set of customers. The firm gains competitive advantage from how it configures the value chain, or the set of activities involved in creating, producing, selling, delivering, and supporting its products or services. For decades businesspeople have studied positioning and the best ways to design activities and integrate them. However, companies have overlooked opportunities to meet fundamental societal needs and misunderstood how societal harms and weaknesses affect value chains. Our field of vision has simply been too narrow.

In understanding the business environment, managers have focused most of their attention on the industry, or the particular business in which the firm competes. This is because industry structure has a decisive impact on a firm's profitability. What has been missed, however, is the profound effect that location can have on productivity and innovation. Companies have failed to grasp the importance of the broader business environment surrounding their major operations.

How Shared Value Is Created

Companies can create economic value by creating societal value. There are three distinct ways to do this: by reconceiving products and markets, redefining productivity in the value chain, and building supportive industry clusters at the company's locations. Each of these is part of the virtuous circle of shared value; improving value in one area gives rise to opportunities in the others.

The concept of shared value resets the boundaries of capitalism. By better connecting companies' success with societal improvement, it opens up many ways to serve new needs, gain efficiency, create differentiation, and expand markets.

The ability to create shared value applies equally to advanced economies and developing countries, though the specific opportunities will differ. The opportunities will also differ markedly across industries and companies—but every company has them. And their range and scope is far broader than has been recognized. (The idea of shared value was initially explored in a December 2006 HBR article by Michael E. Porter and Mark R. Kramer, "Strategy and Society: The Link Between Competitive Advantage and Corporate Social Responsibility.")

Reconceiving Products and Markets

Society's needs are huge—health, better housing, improved nutrition, help for the aging, greater financial security, less environmental damage. Arguably, they are the greatest unmet needs in the global economy. In business we have spent decades learning how to parse and manufacture demand while missing the most important demand of all. Too many companies have lost sight of that most basic of questions: Is our product good for our customers? Or for our customers' customers?

In advanced economies, demand for products and services that meet societal needs is rapidly growing. Food companies that traditionally concentrated on taste and quantity to drive more and more consumption are refocusing on the fundamental need for better nutrition. Intel and IBM are both devising ways to help utilities harness digital intelligence in order to economize on power usage. Wells Fargo has developed a line of products and tools that help customers budget, manage credit, and pay down debt. Sales of GE's Ecomagination products reached $18 billion in 2009—the size of a *Fortune* 150

Blurring the Profit/Nonprofit Boundary

THE CONCEPT OF SHARED VALUE blurs the line between for-profit and nonprofit organizations. New kinds of hybrid enterprises are rapidly appearing. For example, WaterHealth International, a fast-growing for-profit, uses innovative water purification techniques to distribute clean water at minimal cost to more than one million people in rural India, Ghana, and the Philippines. Its investors include not only the socially focused Acumen Fund and the International Finance Corporation of the World Bank but also Dow Chemical's venture fund. Revolution Foods, a four-year-old venture-capital-backed U.S. start-up, provides 60,000 fresh, healthful, and nutritious meals to students daily—and does so at a higher gross margin than traditional competitors. Waste Concern, a hybrid profit/nonprofit enterprise started in Bangladesh 15 years ago, has built the capacity to convert 700 tons of trash, collected daily from neighborhood slums, into organic fertilizer, thereby increasing crop yields and reducing CO_2 emissions. Seeded with capital from the Lions Club and the United Nations Development Programme, the company improves health conditions while earning a substantial gross margin through fertilizer sales and carbon credits.

The blurring of the boundary between successful for-profits and nonprofits is one of the strong signs that creating shared value is possible.

---

company. GE now predicts that revenues of Ecomagination products will grow at twice the rate of total company revenues over the next five years.

In these and many other ways, whole new avenues for innovation open up, and shared value is created. Society's gains are even greater, because businesses will often be far more effective than governments and nonprofits are at marketing that motivates customers to embrace products and services that create societal benefits, like healthier food or environmentally friendly products.

Equal or greater opportunities arise from serving disadvantaged communities and developing countries. Though societal needs are even more pressing there, these communities have not been recognized as viable markets. Today attention is riveted on India, China, and, increasingly, Brazil, which offer firms the prospect of reaching billions of new customers at the bottom of the pyramid—a notion persuasively articulated by C. K. Prahalad. Yet these countries have always had huge needs, as do many developing countries.

Similar opportunities await in nontraditional communities in advanced countries. We have learned, for example, that poor urban areas are America's most underserved market; their substantial concentrated purchasing power has often been overlooked. (See the research of the Initiative for a Competitive Inner City, at icic.org.)

The societal benefits of providing appropriate products to lower-income and disadvantaged consumers can be profound, while the profits for companies can be substantial. For example, low-priced cell phones that provide mobile banking services are helping the poor save money securely and transforming the ability of small farmers to produce and market their crops. In Kenya, Vodafone's M-PESA mobile banking service signed up 10 million customers in three years; the funds it handles now represent 11% of that country's GDP. In India, Thomson Reuters has developed a promising monthly service for farmers who earn an average of $2,000 a year. For a fee of $5 a quarter, it provides weather and crop-pricing information and agricultural advice. The service reaches an estimated 2 million farmers, and early research indicates that it has helped increase the incomes of more than 60% of them—in some cases even tripling incomes. As capitalism begins to work in poorer communities, new opportunities for economic development and social progress increase exponentially.

For a company, the starting point for creating this kind of shared value is to identify all the societal needs, benefits, and harms that are or could be embodied in the firm's products. The opportunities are not static; they change constantly as technology evolves, economies develop, and societal priorities shift. An ongoing exploration of societal needs will lead companies to discover new opportunities for differentiation and repositioning in traditional markets, and to recognize the potential of new markets they previously overlooked.

Meeting needs in underserved markets often requires redesigned products or different distribution methods. These requirements can trigger fundamental innovations that also have application in traditional markets. Microfinance, for example, was invented to serve unmet financing needs in developing countries. Now it is growing rapidly in the United States, where it is filling an important gap that was unrecognized.

Redefining Productivity in the Value Chain

A company's value chain inevitably affects—and is affected by—numerous societal issues, such as natural resource and water use, health and safety, working conditions, and equal treatment in the workplace. Opportunities to create shared value arise because societal problems can create economic costs in the firm's value chain. Many so-called externalities actually inflict internal costs on the firm, even in the absence of regulation or resource taxes. Excess packaging of products and greenhouse gases are not just costly to the environment but costly to the business. Walmart, for example, was able to address both issues by reducing its packaging and rerouting its trucks to cut 100 million miles from its delivery routes in 2009, saving $200 million even as it shipped more products. Innovation in disposing of plastic used in stores has saved millions in lower disposal costs to landfills.

The new thinking reveals that the congruence between societal progress and productivity in the value chain is far greater than traditionally believed (see the sidebar "The Connection Between Competitive Advantage and Social Issues"). The synergy increases when firms approach societal issues from a shared value perspective and invent new ways of operating to address them. So far, however, few companies have reaped the full productivity benefits in areas such as health, safety, environmental performance, and employee retention and capability.

But there are unmistakable signs of change. Efforts to minimize pollution were once thought to inevitably increase business costs—and to occur only because of regulation and taxes. Today there is a growing consensus that major improvements in environmental performance can often be achieved with better technology at nominal incremental cost and can even yield net cost savings through enhanced resource utilization, process efficiency, and quality.

The Connection Between Competitive Advantage and Social Issues

THERE ARE NUMEROUS WAYS in which addressing societal concerns can yield productivity benefits to a firm. Consider, for example, what happens when a firm invests in a wellness program. Society benefits because employees and their families become healthier, and the firm minimizes employee absences and lost productivity. The graphic below depicts some areas where the connections are strongest.

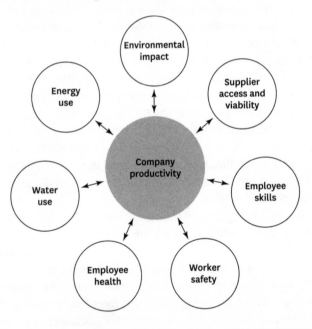

In each of the areas in the sidebar, a deeper understanding of productivity and a growing awareness of the fallacy of short-term cost reductions (which often actually lower productivity or make it unsustainable) are giving rise to new approaches. The following are some of the most important ways in which shared value thinking is transforming the value chain, which are not independent but often mutually reinforcing. Efforts in these and other areas are still works in process, whose implications will be felt for years to come.

Energy use and logistics

The use of energy throughout the value chain is being reexamined, whether it be in processes, transportation, buildings, supply chains, distribution channels, or support services. Triggered by energy price spikes and a new awareness of opportunities for energy efficiency, this reexamination was under way even before carbon emissions became a global focus. The result has been striking improvements in energy utilization through better technology, recycling, cogeneration, and numerous other practices—all of which create shared value.

We are learning that shipping is expensive, not just because of energy costs and emissions but because it adds time, complexity, inventory costs, and management costs. Logistical systems are beginning to be redesigned to reduce shipping distances, streamline handling, improve vehicle routing, and the like. All of these steps create shared value. The British retailer Marks & Spencer's ambitious overhaul of its supply chain, for example, which involves steps as simple as stopping the purchase of supplies from one hemisphere to ship to another, is expected to save the retailer £175 million annually by fiscal 2016, while hugely reducing carbon emissions. In the process of reexamining logistics, thinking about outsourcing and location will also be revised (as we will discuss).

Resource use

Heightened environmental awareness and advances in technology are catalyzing new approaches in areas such as utilization of water, raw materials, and packaging, as well as expanding recycling and reuse. The opportunities apply to all resources, not just those that have been identified by environmentalists. Better resource utilization—enabled by improving technology—will permeate all parts of the value chain and will spread to suppliers and channels. Landfills will fill more slowly.

For example, Coca-Cola has already reduced its worldwide water consumption by 9% from a 2004 baseline—nearly halfway to its goal of a 20% reduction by 2012. Dow Chemical managed to reduce consumption of fresh water at its largest production site by one billion gallons—enough water to supply nearly 40,000 people in the U.S. for a year—resulting in savings of $4 million. The demand for water-saving technology has allowed India's Jain Irrigation, a leading global manufacturer of complete drip irrigation systems for water conservation, to achieve a 41% compound annual growth rate in revenue over the past five years.

Procurement

The traditional playbook calls for companies to commoditize and exert maximum bargaining power on suppliers to drive down prices—even when purchasing from small businesses or subsistence-level farmers. More recently, firms have been rapidly outsourcing to suppliers in lower-wage locations.

Today some companies are beginning to understand that marginalized suppliers cannot remain productive or sustain, much less improve, their quality. By increasing access to inputs, sharing technology, and providing financing, companies can improve supplier quality and productivity while ensuring access to growing volume. Improving productivity will often trump lower prices. As suppliers get stronger, their environmental impact often falls dramatically, which further improves their efficiency. Shared value is created.

A good example of such new procurement thinking can be found at Nespresso, one of Nestlé's fastest-growing divisions, which has enjoyed annual growth of 30% since 2000. Nespresso combines a sophisticated espresso machine with single-cup aluminum capsules containing ground coffees from around the world. Offering quality and convenience, Nespresso has expanded the market for premium coffee.

Obtaining a reliable supply of specialized coffees is extremely challenging, however. Most coffees are grown by small farmers in impoverished rural areas of Africa and Latin America, who are trapped in a cycle of low productivity, poor quality, and environmental degradation that limits production volume. To address these issues, Nestlé redesigned procurement. It worked intensively with its growers, providing advice on farming practices, guaranteeing bank loans, and helping secure inputs such as plant stock, pesticides, and fertilizers.

The Role of Social Entrepreneurs

BUSINESSES ARE NOT THE ONLY PLAYERS in finding profitable solutions to social problems. A whole generation of social entrepreneurs is pioneering new product concepts that meet social needs using viable business models. Because they are not locked into narrow traditional business thinking, social entrepreneurs are often well ahead of established corporations in discovering these opportunities. Social enterprises that create shared value can scale up far more rapidly than purely social programs, which often suffer from an inability to grow and become self-sustaining.

Real social entrepreneurship should be measured by its ability to create shared value, not just social benefit.

Nestlé established local facilities to measure the quality of the coffee at the point of purchase, which allowed it to pay a premium for better beans directly to the growers and thus improve their incentives. Greater yield per hectare and higher production quality increased growers' incomes, and the environmental impact of farms shrank. Meanwhile, Nestlé's reliable supply of good coffee grew significantly. Shared value was created.

Embedded in the Nestlé example is a far broader insight, which is the advantage of buying from capable local suppliers. Outsourcing to other locations and countries creates transaction costs and inefficiencies that can offset lower wage and input costs. Capable local suppliers help firms avoid these costs and can reduce cycle time, increase flexibility, foster faster learning, and enable innovation. Buying local includes not only local companies but also local units of national or international companies. When firms buy locally, their suppliers can get stronger, increase their profits, hire more people, and pay better wages—all of which will benefit other businesses in the community. Shared value is created.

Distribution

Companies are beginning to reexamine distribution practices from a shared value perspective. As iTunes, Kindle, and Google Scholar (which offers texts of scholarly literature online) demonstrate, profitable new distribution models can also dramatically reduce paper and plastic usage. Similarly, microfinance has created a cost-efficient new model of distributing financial services to small businesses.

Opportunities for new distribution models can be even greater in nontraditional markets. For example, Hindustan Unilever is creating a new direct-to-home distribution system, run by underprivileged female entrepreneurs, in Indian villages of fewer than 2,000 people. Unilever provides microcredit and training and now has more than 45,000 entrepreneurs covering some 100,000 villages across 15 Indian states. Project Shakti, as this distribution system is called, benefits communities not only by giving women skills that often double their household income but also by reducing the spread of communicable diseases through increased access to hygiene products. This is a good example of how the unique ability of business to market to hard-to-reach consumers can benefit society by getting life-altering products into the hands of people that need them. Project Shakti now accounts for 5% of Unilever's total revenues in India and has extended the company's reach into rural areas and built its brand in media-dark regions, creating major economic value for the company.

Employee productivity

The focus on holding down wage levels, reducing benefits, and offshoring is beginning to give way to an awareness of the positive effects that a living wage, safety, wellness, training, and opportunities for advancement for employees have on productivity. Many companies, for example, traditionally sought to minimize the cost of "expensive" employee health care coverage or even eliminate health coverage altogether. Today leading companies have learned that because of lost workdays and diminished employee productivity, poor health costs them more than health benefits do. Take Johnson & Johnson. By helping employees stop smoking (a two-thirds reduction in the past 15 years) and implementing numerous other wellness programs, the company has saved $250 million on health care costs, a return of $2.71 for every dollar spent on wellness from 2002 to 2008. Moreover, Johnson & Johnson has benefited from a more present and productive workforce. If labor unions focused more on shared value, too, these kinds of employee approaches would spread even faster.

Location

Business thinking has embraced the myth that location no longer matters, because logistics are inexpensive, information flows rapidly, and markets are global. The cheaper the location, then, the better. Concern about the local communities in which a company operates has faded.

That oversimplified thinking is now being challenged, partly by the rising costs of energy and carbon emissions but also by a greater recognition of the productivity cost of highly dispersed production systems and the hidden costs of distant procurement discussed earlier. Walmart, for example, is increasingly sourcing produce for its food sections from local farms near its warehouses. It has discovered that the savings on transportation costs and the ability to restock in smaller quantities more than offset the lower prices of industrial farms farther away. Nestlé is establishing smaller plants closer to its markets and stepping up efforts to maximize the use of locally available materials.

The calculus of locating activities in developing countries is also changing. Olam International, a leading cashew producer, traditionally shipped its nuts from Africa to Asia for processing at facilities staffed by productive Asian workers. But by opening local processing plants and training workers in Tanzania, Mozambique, Nigeria, and Côte d'Ivoire, Olam has cut processing and shipping costs by as much as 25%—not to mention, greatly reduced carbon emissions. In making this move, Olam also built preferred relationships with local farmers. And it has provided direct employment to 17,000 people—95% of whom are women—and indirect employment to an equal number of people, in rural areas where jobs otherwise were not available.

These trends may well lead companies to remake their value chains by moving some activities closer to home and having fewer major production locations. Until now, many companies have thought that being global meant moving production to locations with the lowest labor costs and designing their supply chains to achieve the most immediate impact on expenses. In reality, the strongest international competitors will often be those that can establish deeper roots in important communities. Companies that can embrace this new locational thinking will create shared value.

As these examples illustrate, reimagining value chains from the perspective of shared value will offer significant new ways to innovate and unlock new economic value that most businesses have missed.

Enabling Local Cluster Development

No company is self-contained. The success of every company is affected by the supporting companies and infrastructure around it. Productivity and innovation are strongly influenced by "clusters," or geographic concentrations of firms, related businesses, suppliers, service providers, and logistical infrastructure in a particular field—such as IT in Silicon Valley, cut flowers in Kenya, and diamond cutting in Surat, India.

Clusters include not only businesses but institutions such as academic programs, trade associations, and standards organizations. They also draw on the broader public assets in the surrounding community, such as schools and universities, clean water, fair-competition laws, quality standards, and market transparency.

Clusters are prominent in all successful and growing regional economies and play a crucial role in driving productivity, innovation, and competitiveness. Capable local suppliers foster greater logistical efficiency and ease of collaboration, as we have discussed. Stronger local capabilities in areas such as training, transportation services, and related industries also boost productivity. Without a supporting cluster, conversely, productivity suffers.

Deficiencies in the framework conditions surrounding the cluster also create internal costs for firms. Poor public education imposes productivity and remedial-training costs. Poor transportation infrastructure drives up the costs of logistics. Gender or racial discrimination reduces the pool of capable employees. Poverty limits the demand for products and leads to environmental degradation, unhealthy workers, and high security costs. As companies have increasingly become disconnected from their communities, however, their influence in solving these problems has waned even as their costs have grown.

Firms create shared value by building clusters to improve company productivity while addressing gaps or failures in the framework conditions surrounding the cluster. Efforts to develop or attract capable suppliers, for example, enable the procurement benefits we discussed earlier. A focus on clusters and location has been all but absent in management thinking. Cluster thinking has also been missing in many economic development initiatives, which have failed because they involved isolated interventions and overlooked critical complementary investments.

A key aspect of cluster building in developing and developed countries alike is the formation of open and transparent markets. In inefficient or monopolized markets where workers are exploited, where suppliers do not receive fair prices, and where price transparency is lacking, productivity suffers. Enabling fair and open markets, which is often best done in conjunction with partners, can allow a company to secure reliable supplies and give suppliers better incentives for quality and efficiency while also substantially improving the incomes and purchasing power of local citizens. A positive cycle of economic and social development results.

When a firm builds clusters in its key locations, it also amplifies the connection between its success and its communities' success. A firm's growth has multiplier effects, as jobs are created in supporting industries, new companies are seeded, and demand for ancillary services rises. A company's efforts to improve framework conditions for the cluster spill over to other participants and the local economy. Workforce development initiatives, for example, increase the supply of skilled employees for many other firms as well.

At Nespresso, Nestlé also worked to build clusters, which made its new procurement practices far more effective. It set out to

Creating Shared Value: Implications for Government and Civil Society

WHILE OUR FOCUS HERE is primarily on companies, the principles of shared value apply equally to governments and nonprofit organizations.

Governments and NGOs will be most effective if they think in value terms—considering benefits relative to costs—and focus on the results achieved rather than the funds and effort expended. Activists have tended to approach social improvement from an ideological or absolutist perspective, as if social benefits should be pursued at any cost. Governments and NGOs often assume that trade-offs between economic and social benefits are inevitable, exacerbating these trade-offs through their approaches. For example, much environmental regulation still takes the form of command-and-control mandates and enforcement actions designed to embarrass and punish companies.

Regulators would accomplish much more by focusing on measuring environmental performance and introducing standards, phase-in periods, and support for technology that would promote innovation, improve the environment, and increase competitiveness simultaneously.

The principle of shared value creation cuts across the traditional divide between the responsibilities of business and those of government or civil society. From society's perspective, it does not matter what types of organizations created the value. What matters is that benefits are delivered by those organizations—or combinations of organizations—that are best positioned to achieve the most impact for the least cost. Finding ways to boost productivity is equally valuable whether in the service of commercial or societal objectives. In short, the principle of value creation should guide the use of resources across all areas of societal concern.

Fortunately, a new type of NGO has emerged that understands the importance of productivity and value creation. Such organizations have often had a remarkable impact. One example is TechnoServe, which has partnered with

build agricultural, technical, financial, and logistical firms and capabilities in each coffee region, to further support efficiency and high-quality local production. Nestlé led efforts to increase access to essential agricultural inputs such as plant stock, fertilizers, and irrigation equipment; strengthen regional farmer co-ops by helping them finance shared wet-milling facilities for both regional and global corporations to promote the development of competitive agricultural clusters in more than 30 countries. Root Capital accomplishes a similar objective by providing financing to farmers and businesses that are too large for microfinance but too small for normal bank financing. Since 2000, Root Capital has lent more than $200 million to 282 businesses, through which it has reached 400,000 farmers and artisans. It has financed the cultivation of 1.4 million acres of organic agriculture in Latin America and Africa. Root Capital regularly works with corporations, utilizing future purchase orders as collateral for its loans to farmers and helping to strengthen corporate supply chains and improve the quality of purchased inputs.

Some private foundations have begun to see the power of working with businesses to create shared value. The Bill & Melinda Gates Foundation, for example, has formed partnerships with leading global corporations to foster agricultural clusters in developing countries. The foundation carefully focuses on commodities where climate and soil conditions give a particular region a true competitive advantage. The partnerships bring in NGOs like TechnoServe and Root Capital, as well as government officials, to work on precompetitive issues that improve the cluster and upgrade the value chain for all participants. This approach recognizes that helping small farmers increase their yields will not create any lasting benefits unless there are ready buyers for their crops, other enterprises that can process the crops once they are harvested, and a local cluster that includes efficient logistical infrastructure, input availability, and the like. The active engagement of corporations is essential to mobilizing these elements.

Forward-thinking foundations can also serve as honest brokers and allay fears by mitigating power imbalances between small local enterprises, NGOs, governments, and companies. Such efforts will require a new assumption that shared value can come only as a result of effective collaboration among all parties.

producing higher-quality beans; and support an extension program to advise all farmers on growing techniques. It also worked in partnership with the Rainforest Alliance, a leading international NGO, to teach farmers more-sustainable practices that make production volumes more reliable. In the process, Nestlé's productivity improved.

How Shared Value Differs from Corporate Social Responsibility

CREATING SHARED VALUE (CSV) should supersede corporate social responsibility (CSR) in guiding the investments of companies in their communities. CSR programs focus mostly on reputation and have only a limited connection to the business, making them hard to justify and maintain over the long run. In contrast, CSV is integral to a company's profitability and competitive position. It leverages the unique resources and expertise of the company to create economic value by creating social value.

CSR	CSV
• Values: doing good	• Value: economic and societal benefits relative to cost
• Citizenship, philanthropy, sustainability	• Joint company and community value creation
• Discretionary or in response to external pressure	• Integral to competing
• Separate from profit maximization	• Integral to profit maximization
• Agenda is determined by external reporting and personal preferences	• Agenda is company-specific and internally generated
• Impact limited by corporate footprint and CSR budget	• Realigns the entire company budget
Example: Fair trade purchasing	*Example:* Transforming procurement to increase quality and yield

In both cases, compliance with laws and ethical standards and reducing harm from corporate activities are assumed.

A good example of a company working to improve framework conditions in its cluster is Yara, the world's largest mineral fertilizer company. Yara realized that the lack of logistical infrastructure in many parts of Africa was preventing farmers from gaining efficient access to fertilizers and other essential agricultural inputs, and from transporting their crops efficiently to market. Yara is tackling this problem through a $60 million investment in a program to improve ports and roads, which is designed to create agricultural growth corridors in Mozambique and Tanzania. The company is working on this initiative with local governments and support from the Norwegian government. In Mozambique alone, the corridor is expected to benefit more than 200,000 small farmers and create 350,000 new jobs. The improvements will help Yara grow its business but will support the whole agricultural cluster, creating huge multiplier effects.

The benefits of cluster building apply not only in emerging economies but also in advanced countries. North Carolina's Research Triangle is a notable example of public and private collaboration that has created shared value by developing clusters in such areas as information technology and life sciences. That region, which has benefited from continued investment from both the private sector and local government, has experienced huge growth in employment, incomes, and company performance, and has fared better than most during the downturn.

To support cluster development in the communities in which they operate, companies need to identify gaps and deficiencies in areas such as logistics, suppliers, distribution channels, training, market organization, and educational institutions. Then the task is to focus on the weaknesses that represent the greatest constraints to the company's own productivity and growth, and distinguish those areas that the company is best equipped to influence directly from those in which collaboration is more cost-effective. Here is where the shared value opportunities will be greatest. Initiatives that address cluster weaknesses that constrain companies will be much more effective than community-focused corporate social responsibility programs, which often have limited impact because they take on too many areas without focusing on value.

But efforts to enhance infrastructure and institutions in a region often require collective action, as the Nestlé, Yara, and Research Triangle examples show. Companies should try to enlist partners to share the cost, win support, and assemble the right skills. The most successful cluster development programs are ones that involve collaboration within the private sector, as well as trade associations, government agencies, and NGOs.

Government Regulation and Shared Value

THE RIGHT KIND OF GOVERNMENT REGULATION can encourage companies to pursue shared value; the wrong kind works against it and even makes trade-offs between economic and social goals inevitable.

Regulation is necessary for well-functioning markets, something that became abundantly clear during the recent financial crisis. However, the ways in which regulations are designed and implemented determine whether they benefit society or work against it.

Regulations that enhance shared value set goals and stimulate innovation. They highlight a societal objective and create a level playing field to encourage companies to invest in shared value rather than maximize short-term profit. Such regulations have a number of characteristics:

First, they set clear and measurable social goals, whether they involve energy use, health matters, or safety. Where appropriate, they set prices for resources (such as water) that reflect true costs. Second, they set performance standards but do not prescribe the methods to achieve them—those are left to companies. Third, they define phase-in periods for meeting standards, which reflect the investment or new-product cycle in the industry. Phase-in periods give companies time to develop and introduce new products and processes in a way consistent with the economics of their business. Fourth, they put in place universal measurement and performance-reporting systems, with government investing in infrastructure for collecting reliable benchmarking

Creating Shared Value in Practice

Not all profit is equal—an idea that has been lost in the narrow, short-term focus of financial markets and in much management thinking. Profits involving a social purpose represent a higher form of capitalism—one that will enable society to advance more rapidly while allowing companies to grow even more. The result is a positive cycle of company and community prosperity, which leads to profits that endure.

Creating shared value presumes compliance with the law and ethical standards, as well as mitigating any harm caused by the business, but goes far beyond that. The opportunity to create economic value through creating societal value will be one of the most powerful forces driving growth in the global economy. This thinking represents a new way of understanding customers, productivity, and the data (such as nutritional deficiencies in each community). This motivates and enables continual improvement beyond current targets. Finally, appropriate regulations require efficient and timely reporting of results, which can then be audited by the government as necessary, rather than impose detailed and expensive compliance processes on everyone.

Regulation that discourages shared value looks very different. it forces compliance with particular practices, rather than focusing on measurable social improvement. It mandates a particular approach to meeting a standard—blocking innovation and almost always inflicting cost on companies. When governments fall into the trap of this sort of regulation, they undermine the very progress that they seek while triggering fierce resistance from business that slows progress further and blocks shared value that would improve competitiveness.

To be sure, companies locked into the old mind-set will resist even well-constructed regulation. As shared value principles become more widely accepted, however, business and government will become more aligned on regulation in many areas. Companies will come to understand that the right kind of regulation can actually foster economic value creation.

Finally, regulation will be needed to limit the pursuit of exploitative, unfair, or deceptive practices in which companies benefit at the expense of society. Strict antitrust policy, for example, is essential to ensure that the benefits of company success flow to customers, suppliers, and workers.

external influences on corporate success. It highlights the immense human needs to be met, the large new markets to serve, and the internal costs of social and community deficits—as well as the competitive advantages available from addressing them. Until recently, companies have simply not approached their businesses this way.

Creating shared value will be more effective and far more sustainable than the majority of today's corporate efforts in the social arena. Companies will make real strides on the environment, for example, when they treat it as a productivity driver rather than a feel-good response to external pressure. Or consider access to housing. A shared value approach would have led financial services companies to create innovative products that prudently increased access to home ownership. This was recognized by the Mexican construction company Urbi, which pioneered a mortgage-financing "rent-to-own" plan. Major U.S. banks, in contrast, promoted unsustainable financing vehicles that turned out to be socially and economically devastating, while claiming they were socially responsible because they had charitable contribution programs.

Inevitably, the most fertile opportunities for creating shared value will be closely related to a company's particular business, and in areas most important to the business. Here a company can benefit the most economically and hence sustain its commitment over time. Here is also where a company brings the most resources to bear, and where its scale and market presence equip it to have a meaningful impact on a societal problem.

Ironically, many of the shared value pioneers have been those with more-limited resources—social entrepreneurs and companies in developing countries. These outsiders have been able to see the opportunities more clearly. In the process, the distinction between for-profits and nonprofits is blurring.

Shared value is defining a whole new set of best practices that all companies must embrace. It will also become an integral part of strategy. The essence of strategy is choosing a unique positioning and a distinctive value chain to deliver on it. Shared value opens up many new needs to meet, new products to offer, new customers to serve, and new ways to configure the value chain. And the competitive advantages that arise from creating shared value will often be more sustainable than conventional cost and quality improvements. The cycle of imitation and zero-sum competition can be broken.

The opportunities to create shared value are widespread and growing. Not every company will have them in every area, but our experience has been that companies discover more and more opportunities over time as their line operating units grasp this concept. It has taken a decade, but GE's Ecomagination initiative, for example, is now producing a stream of fast-growing products and services across the company.

A shared value lens can be applied to every major company decision. Could our product design incorporate greater social benefits? Are we serving all the communities that would benefit from our products? Do our processes and logistical approaches maximize efficiencies in energy and water use? Could our new plant be constructed in a way that achieves greater community impact? How are gaps in our cluster holding back our efficiency and speed of innovation? How could we enhance our community as a business location? If sites are comparable economically, at which one will the local community benefit the most? If a company can improve societal conditions, it will often improve business conditions and thereby trigger positive feedback loops.

The three avenues for creating shared value are mutually reinforcing. Enhancing the cluster, for example, will enable more local procurement and less dispersed supply chains. New products and services that meet social needs or serve overlooked markets will require new value chain choices in areas such as production, marketing, and distribution. And new value chain configurations will create demand for equipment and technology that save energy, conserve resources, and support employees.

Creating shared value will require concrete and tailored metrics for each business unit in each of the three areas. While some companies have begun to track various social impacts, few have yet tied them to their economic interests at the business level.

Shared value creation will involve new and heightened forms of collaboration. While some shared value opportunities are possible for a company to seize on its own, others will benefit from insights, skills, and resources that cut across profit/nonprofit and private/public boundaries. Here, companies will be less successful if they attempt to tackle societal problems on their own, especially those involving cluster development. Major competitors may also need to work together on precompetitive framework conditions, something that has not been common in reputation-driven CSR initiatives. Successful collaboration will be data driven, clearly linked to defined outcomes, well connected to the goals of all stakeholders, and tracked with clear metrics.

Governments and NGOs can enable and reinforce shared value or work against it. (For more on this topic, see the sidebar "Government Regulation and Shared Value.")

The Next Evolution in Capitalism

Shared value holds the key to unlocking the next wave of business innovation and growth. It will also reconnect company success and community success in ways that have been lost in an age of narrow management approaches, short-term thinking, and deepening divides among society's institutions.

Shared value focuses companies on the right kind of profits—profits that create societal benefits rather than diminish them. Capital markets will undoubtedly continue to pressure companies to generate short-term profits, and some companies will surely continue to reap profits at the expense of societal needs. But such profits will often prove to be short-lived, and far greater opportunities will be missed.

The moment for an expanded view of value creation has come. A host of factors, such as the growing social awareness of employees and citizens and the increased scarcity of natural resources, will drive unprecedented opportunities to create shared value.

We need a more sophisticated form of capitalism, one imbued with a social purpose. But that purpose should arise not out of charity but out of a deeper understanding of competition and economic value creation. This next evolution in the capitalist model recognizes new and better ways to develop products, serve markets, and build productive enterprises.

Creating shared value represents a broader conception of Adam Smith's invisible hand. It opens the doors of the pin factory to a wider set of influences. It is not philanthropy but self-interested behavior to create economic value by creating societal value. If all companies individually pursued shared value connected to their particular businesses, society's overall interests would be served. And companies would acquire legitimacy in the eyes of the communities in which they operated, which would allow democracy to work as governments set policies that fostered and supported business. Survival of the fittest would still prevail, but market competition would benefit society in ways we have lost.

Creating shared value represents a new approach to managing that cuts across disciplines. Because of the traditional divide between economic concerns and social ones, people in the public and private sectors have often followed very different educational and career paths. As a result, few managers have the understanding of social and environmental issues required to move beyond today's CSR approaches, and few social sector leaders have the managerial training and entrepreneurial mind-set needed to design and implement shared value models. Most business schools still teach the narrow view of capitalism, even though more and more of their graduates hunger for a greater sense of purpose and a growing number are drawn to social entrepreneurship. The results have been missed opportunity and public cynicism.

Business school curricula will need to broaden in a number of areas. For example, the efficient use and stewardship of all forms of resources will define the next-generation thinking on value chains. Customer behavior and marketing courses will have to move beyond persuasion and demand creation to the study of deeper human needs and how to serve nontraditional customer groups. Clusters, and the broader locational influences on company productivity and innovation, will form a new core discipline in business schools; economic development will no longer be left only to public policy and economics departments. Business and government courses will examine the economic impact of societal factors on enterprises, moving beyond the effects of regulation and macroeconomics. And finance will need to rethink how capital markets can actually support true value creation in companies—their fundamental purpose—not just benefit financial market participants.

There is nothing soft about the concept of shared value. These proposed changes in business school curricula are not qualitative and do not depart from economic value creation. Instead, they represent the next stage in our understanding of markets, competition, and business management.

Not all societal problems can be solved through shared value solutions. But shared value offers corporations the opportunity to utilize their skills, resources, and management capability to lead social progress in ways that even the best-intentioned governmental and social sector organizations can rarely match. In the process, businesses can earn the respect of society again.

Originally published in January–February 2011. Reprint R1101C

About the Contributors

JAMES ALLEN is a partner in Bain & Company's London office and a cohead of the firm's global strategy practice. He also leads Bain's Founder's Mentality 100 initiative. He is a coauthor of a number of best-selling books including *Profit from the Core* (Harvard Business Review Press, 2010) and *The Founder's Mentality: How to Overcome the Predictable Crises of Growth* (Harvard Business Review Press, June 2016).

STEVE BLANK is an adjunct professor at Stanford University, a senior fellow at Columbia University, and a lecturer at the University of California, Berkeley. He has been either a cofounder or an early employee at eight high-tech startups, and he helped start the National Science Foundation Innovation Corps and the Hacking for Defense and Hacking for Diplomacy programs. He blogs at www.steveblank.com.

ADAM BRANDENBURGER holds positions as the J. P. Valles Professor at the Stern School of Business, Distinguished Professor at the Tandon School of Engineering, and faculty director of the Program on Creativity and Innovation at NYU Shanghai, all at New York University.

IVY BUCHE is an associate director of the Business Transformation Initiative at IMD.

SANGEET PAUL CHOUDARY is a C-level adviser on platform business models to executives around the world and an entrepreneur-in-residence at INSEAD. He has been ranked among the top 30 emerging business thinkers globally by Thinkers50 and selected as a Young Global Leader by the World Economic Forum. He is a coauthor of *Platform Revolution*. Follow him on Twitter @sanguit.

CLAYTON M. CHRISTENSEN is the Kim B. Clark Professor of Business Administration at Harvard Business School and a coauthor of *The Prosperity Paradox: How Innovation Can Lift Nations Out of Poverty*.

CHARLES DHANARAJ is the H. F. Gerry Lenfest Professor of Strategy at Temple University's Fox School of Business, where he is also the founding executive director of the Translational Research Center.

ROBERT S. KAPLAN is a senior fellow and the Marvin Bower Professor of Leadership Development, Emeritus, at Harvard Business School. He is a coauthor, with Michael E. Porter, of "How to Solve the Cost Crisis in Health Care" (*Harvard Business Review*, September 2011).

MARK R. KRAMER is a senior lecturer at Harvard Business School and a cofounder and a managing director of FSG, a global social-impact consulting firm.

A.G. LAFLEY, the retired CEO of Procter & Gamble, serves on the board of Snap Inc.

CLAIRE LOVE is a New York-based project leader at Boston Consulting Group's Strategy Institute.

THOMAS W. MALNIGHT is a professor of strategy and the faculty director of the Business Transformation Initiative at IMD in Lausanne, Switzerland. He is a coauthor of *Ready? The 3Rs of Preparing Your Organization for the Future*.

ROGER L. MARTIN is the director of the Martin Prosperity Institute and a former dean of the Rotman School of Management at the University of Toronto. He is a coauthor of *Creating Great Choices: A Leader's Guide to Integrative Thinking* (Harvard Business Review Press, 2017).

RITA GUNTHER McGRATH, a professor at Columbia Business School, is a globally recognized expert on strategy in uncertain and volatile environments. She is the author of the book *The End of Competitive Advantage* (Harvard Business Review Press, 2013).

ANETTE MIKES is an assistant professor in the accounting and management unit at Harvard Business School.

GEOFFREY G. PARKER is a professor of engineering at Dartmouth College and a research fellow at MIT's Initiative on the Digital Economy. He coauthored the book *Platform Revolution* and the October 2006 *Harvard Business Review* article "Strategies for Two-Sided Markets," an HBR all-time top 50 best-seller. Follow him on Twitter @g2parker.

MICHAEL E. PORTER is a university professor at Harvard, based at Harvard Business School in Boston.

MARTIN REEVES is a senior partner and managing director in the Boston Consulting Group's New York office and the director of the BCG Henderson Institute. He is a coauthor of *Your Strategy Needs a Strategy* (Harvard Business Review Press, 2015). Follow him on Twitter @MartinKReeves.

JAN W. RIVKIN is the Bruce V. Rauner Professor at Harvard Business School.

NICOLAJ SIGGELKOW is a professor of management and strategy at the University of Pennsylvania's Wharton School and a codirector of the Mack Institute for Innovation Management. He is a coauthor, with Christian Terwiesch, of *Connected Strategy* (Harvard Business Review Press, 2019).

PHILIPP TILLMANNS is a consultant at Boston Consulting Group in Hamburg and a PhD candidate at RWTH Aachen University in Germany.

MARSHALL W. VAN ALSTYNE is the Questrom Chaired Professor at Boston University School of Business. His work has more than 10,000 citations. He coauthored *Platform Revolution* and the October 2006 *Harvard Business Review* article "Strategies for Two-Sided Markets," an HBR all-time top 50 best-seller. Follow him on Twitter @InfoEcon.

MAXWELL WESSEL is the general manager of SAP.iO, a lecturer at Stanford's Graduate School of Business, and an investor with Next-gen Venture Partners. Follow him on Twitter @maxwellelliot.

CHRIS ZOOK is a partner in Bain & Company's Boston office and has been a cohead of the firm's global strategy practice for twenty years. He is a coauthor of a number of best-selling books including *Profit from the Core* (Harvard Business Review Press, 2010) and *The Founder's Mentality: How to Overcome the Predictable Crises of Growth* (Harvard Business Review Press, June 2016).

Index